Nature's Storyteller

THE LIFE OF
GENE STRATTON-PORTER

BARBARA OLENYIK MORROW

INDIANA HISTORICAL SOCIETY PRESS • INDIANAPOLIS 2010

© 2010 Indiana Historical Society Press

Printed in the United States of America

This book is a publication of the
Indiana Historical Society Press
Eugene and Marilyn Glick Indiana History Center
450 West Ohio Street
Indianapolis, Indiana 46202-3269 USA
www.indianahistory.org
Telephone orders 1-800-447-1830
Fax orders 1-317-234-0562
Online orders @ http://shop.indianahistory.org

The paper in this publication meets the minimum requirements of American National
Standard for Information Sciences—Permanence of Paper for Printed Library Materials,
ANSI Z39. 48–1984

Library of Congress Cataloging-in-Publication Data

Morrow, Barbara Olenyik.
Nature's storyteller : the life of Gene Stratton-Porter / Barbara
Olenyik Morrow.
    p. cm.
Includes bibliographical references and index.
ISBN 978-0-87195-284-4 (cloth : alk. paper)
1. Stratton-Porter, Gene, 1863-1924. 2. Novelists, American—20th
century—Biography. 3. Women naturalists—United States—Biography.
4. Naturalists—United States—Biography. 5. Indiana—Biography. I.
Title.
PS3531.O7345Z68 2010
813'.52—dc22
[B]
                                        2009052653

To my parents, Janet and Robert Olenyik

Nature's Storyteller: The Life of Gene Stratton-Porter is made possible through the generous support of the Lacy Foundation/LDI, Ltd.

CONTENTS

ACKNOWLEDGMENTS

I wish to express my gratitude to numerous people who guided me in writing this biography. I begin with the project managers of two former homes of Gene Stratton-Porter: Randy Lehman and Dave W. Fox. Randy oversees the Limberlost State Historic Site in Geneva, and Dave manages the Wildflower Woods estate—known as the Gene Stratton-Porter State Historic Site—near Rome City. Both generously shared their time and knowledge and fielded my numerous questions. Volunteer Tracy Duncan and gardener Martha Ferguson also aided my research at Wildflower Woods.

I remain indebted to Ken Brunswick, East Central Regional Ecologist for the Indiana Division of Nature Preserves. More than a decade ago, while researching my book *From Ben-Hur to Sister Carrie* (1995), which included a chapter on Stratton-Porter, Ken introduced me to a portion of the former Limberlost Swamp. More recently, Ken led me on another "Limberlost" tour and pointed to progress being made in restoring the region to its former marshy state. Ken also provided the Limberlost map that appears in this book.

Stratton-Porter enthusiast and reenactor Juanita Rapp served as my helpful guide in Wabash County. Along with sharing local lore, she led me to Stratton-Porter's birthplace, the former Hopewell Farm, and pointed out where Gene lived and attended school in the city of Wabash.

Librarians are essential to researchers, and I wish to thank the staffs of the William Henry Smith Memorial Library at the Indiana Historical Society, the Lilly Library at Indiana University, the Cunningham Memorial Library at Indiana State University, the

Bracken Library at Ball State University, the Wabash Carnegie Public Library, the Kendallville Public Library, the Eckhart Public Library in Auburn, and the Geneva branch of the Adams County Public Library. I am especially grateful to Katherine Gould, assistant curator of cultural history at the Indiana State Museum, for help in acquiring the many photographs in this book. Indianapolis film historian and collector Eric Grayson shared his expertise with regard to motion pictures based on Stratton-Porter's novels.

I have been fortunate to have as my editor Ray E. Boomhower, whose talents as an author and as editor of IHS's *Traces of Indiana and Midwestern History* are well-known throughout the Hoosier State and beyond. For all his helpful advice and skillful editing, I offer my sincere thanks.

Finally, thanks goes to my husband Doug, for his patience and unending support.

PROLOGUE

"I live in a world of light, fragrance, beauty and song. No wonder it overflows in my books."

GENE STRATTON-PORTER

In March 1872, when Gene Stratton-Porter was eight years old, President Ulysses S. Grant signed a bill creating America's first national park, Yellowstone. In setting aside that stretch of western wilderness, Congress acted to ensure that everyone, not just a privileged few, could enjoy Yellowstone's natural wonders: the spectacular geysers and hot springs, the thundering waterfalls, and the colorful canyons. Congress also wanted to preserve Yellowstone's natural resources for future generations. Within the huge park were vast evergreen forests, sparkling lakes, and wildlife ranging from bisons to bald eagles. Private developers had already begun ruining the scenic beauty of another natural wonder, Niagara Falls in New York. Congress hoped to spare Yellowstone from similar exploitation.

Growing up on a farm near Wabash, Indiana, Stratton-Porter lived half a continent away from Yellowstone. But even as a young girl, she grasped the importance of protecting and preserving wildlife and wild places. From her mother, she learned how to care for wildflowers and native plants. From her father, she learned how to appreciate wild creatures, especially birds. As an adult, she found the lure of northern Indiana's woodlands and wetlands irresistible and soon discovered her life's work—to share the wonders of the outdoors with others and to urge conservation.

Gene Stratton-Porter believed that to do "strong work any writer must stick to the things he truly knows, the simple, common things of life as he has lived them."

Her tools were her pen and her camera. Over the course of a quarter-century, Stratton-Porter wrote twenty-six books—novels, nonfiction, a collection of essays, children's books, and poetry, all layered and woven with nature lore. Many of the books, as well as the numerous articles she wrote for popular magazines, were lavishly illustrated with photographs she took while exploring the outdoors. Her appeal was enormous and her following vast; her fiction and nonfiction books sold for many years at a rate of nearly seventeen hundred copies a day.

Stratton-Porter enjoyed considerable influence during her career. Some even compared her to President Theodore Roosevelt, who used his high office (1901–09) to protect the nation's forests and natural resources as few politicians ever had. "Each has swayed the millions," author and editor Grant Overton said of Stratton-Porter and Roosevelt in 1923. "Each, beyond all possible question, has influenced human lives." Earlier, in 1921, the prominent scholar and critic William Lyon Phelps made a similar observation about Stratton-Porter: "I have no doubt that she has led millions of boys and girls into the study of natural objects. . . . She is as full of energy as Roosevelt, and as hearty an American." Phelps offered more: "She is a public institution, like Yellowstone Park."

Teddy Roosevelt

Though she wrote for a far-flung audience, Stratton-Porter was, for most of her life, a Hoosier. Her childhood and teenage years were spent in Wabash County. Upon her marriage to Charles Dorwin Porter in 1886, she moved briefly to Decatur in Adams County, then to the neighboring town of Geneva. There, she and Charles built a roomy two-story log home that she named Limberlost Cabin, after the great marshy wilderness located a few miles away. The Limberlost Swamp, with its thirteen thousand acres of bogs, streams, and virgin forest, soon became her outdoor laboratory—the place where she went with notebooks, pencils, and cameras to record, sketch, and photograph the area's vast array of wildlife, especially birds. The swamp, both treacherous and magnificent, also served as her inspiration. It provided the setting for many of her novels and books of natural history.

By 1913, however, her beloved Limberlost was fast disappearing. Developers had moved in, eager to profit from the swamp's timber, oil, and gas resources. For Stratton-Porter, all the logging, dredging, ditching, and road building made it impossible to continue her fieldwork. Searching for a new laboratory, she headed north to Sylvan Lake near Rome City in Noble County, where she had often vacationed. With money from her book sales, she purchased land— eventually 120 acres—along the lakeshore and built an even grander cedar-log home. During the next several years, she worked tirelessly to turn her estate, which she named Wildflower Woods, into a plant and wildlife preserve.

Stratton-Porter's work took on special urgency in 1917 when the Indiana General Assembly passed a law (later repealed) allowing for the drainage of state-owned swampland in Noble and Lagrange counties. Determined to save as many native and rare plants as she could, she motored around the region, loading her seven-passenger automobile

Front and West of Limberlost Cabin (South)
Home of Gene Stratton-Porter

Top: The Cabin at Wildflower Woods on the shores of Sylvan Lake in Rome City, Indiana, built by Stratton-Porter in 1914. **Above:** The Limberlost Cabin in Geneva, Indiana, where Stratton-Porter lived for many years. **Right:** Cover of Stratton-Porter's 1909 novel *A Girl of the Limberlost*.

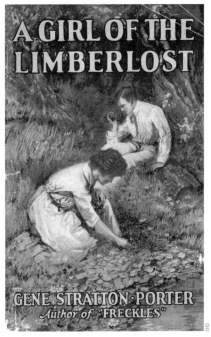

A GIRL OF THE LIMBERLOST

GENE STRATTON-PORTER
Author of "FRECKLES"

with swamp specimens and transplanting them to her property. Eventually, more than seventeen thousand trees, vines, shrubs, and wildflowers were planted at Wildflower Woods, most of them tucked into the soil by her.

In 1919 at age fifty-six, Stratton-Porter was ready for new challenges, and for year-round sunshine. She moved to Southern California, built two more homes, and showed her typical independence by forming her own movie production company. At the time, filmmakers were clamoring to adapt her popular novels into movies. She wanted the movie versions to be every bit as morally uplifting and full of nature lore as her books were. Dissatisfied with Paramount's adaptation of her novel, *Freckles*, in 1917, she decided she could do better and became one of Hollywood's first female producers.

Stratton-Porter threw herself into moviemaking with her usual energy and enthusiasm. "I had a grand time every minute, and gained ten pounds" she said of her experience producing *A Girl of the Limberlost*, based on one of her best-selling novels. But Hollywood's lure was not strong enough to take Stratton-Porter away from her first love: observing, exploring, and chronicling the landscape. She savored the stunning beauty of California's deserts, mountains, and canyons, just as she had earlier reveled in Indiana's forests and marshlands. She also remained at the forefront of an emerging environmental movement. As she had done throughout much of her career, she warned that destroying nature's gifts had dire consequences and she urged collective action. "We, as a nation, have already, in the most wanton and reckless waste the world has ever known, changed our climatic conditions and wasted a good part of our splendid heritage," she wrote in a 1923 column for *McCall's* magazine. "The question now facing us is whether we shall do all that lies in our power to save . . . the spots of natural beauty that remain for our children."

Even at an early age, Stratton-Porter knew that not everyone shared her interest in the outdoors. In 1884, shortly before her twenty-first birthday, she learned how far "out of step" she was with her female peers. "I was considered an outcast and half-demented," she recalled, "because I fished in the rain one night when I might have attended a ball. One woman blasted me with scorn because I had the hardihood to offer to her a timothy straw strung with luscious big, wild red raspberries."

Her reputation as an oddity persisted as Stratton-Porter launched her career. Townsfolk often shook their heads in disbelief as she set off for the woods and swamps clad in high boots and khaki-colored clothes and toting a gun for protection against snakes. Town gossip escalated when she was seen in the company of oil workers and teenaged boys, who told her of unusual wildlife sightings and helped lug her forty pounds of photographic equipment.

Meanwhile, Charles did more than patiently tolerate her career. He often played a supporting role. When his schedule permitted, he accompanied her on her field trips, and when she asked for feedback, he critiqued her writing. Yet their thirty-eight-year marriage was itself not entirely conventional. While most women of that era were dependent on their husbands for financial support, Stratton-Porter grew wealthy from her writings and spent and invested as she pleased. Her move to Wildflower Woods was entirely her own undertaking. Charles, occupied with his business interests in Geneva, visited her on weekends. When she moved to California, he remained in Indiana. As he had done throughout their marriage, he seemed willing to give his wife what she most needed—her freedom.

Stratton-Porter insisted that publishers also grant her considerable freedom. In the early 1900s when she launched her writing career, an educated middle class was on the rise. Americans had more leisure time to read, and they preferred fiction over nonfiction. Stratton-Porter did not think of herself as a novelist. But she quickly recognized that if she crafted a fictional romance, and gave it an outdoor setting, she could share her love of birds, bugs, and blossoms with a wide audience. Doubleday, Page and Company, which became her main publisher, was not convinced. Editors there urged her to cut the "nature stuff" out of her novel *Freckles,* as had publishers who had earlier rejected the manuscript. But Stratton-Porter held firm. She told Doubleday's editors to "make up my work as I think it should be." They did, and after a slow start, *Freckles* (1904) became a hit. Her point proven, Stratton-Porter continued to write "nature stuff" into her fiction.

Because her novels were so popular and profitable, Doubleday, Page yielded to her other requests. Stratton-Porter always preferred writing strictly nature books, where in a conversational, almost chatty style, she shared her unusual and varied experiences with birds and wildlife. Naturalists such as Henry David Thoreau, John Muir, and John Burroughs had established nature writing as a literary genre and had loyal followings of readers. Stratton-Porter hoped that her nonfiction would find an equally devout audience. But compared to her novels, her nature books sold only moderately well—and Doubleday, Page might reasonably have refused to publish her nonfiction. Instead the company did publish her work, with the understanding that each nature book would be followed by a novel. In addition, Doubleday, Page gave Stratton-Porter control over the appearance of her nonfiction, allowing her to select the photographic illustrations and even design the covers. For her novels, she adopted the practice of publishing one every other year on her birthday.

Though she was not passionate about writing fiction, Stratton-Porter nonetheless possessed a gift for storytelling. She knew

Photo of Stratton-Porter in California, circa 1920, by Edward S. Curtis, the famous photographer of the American West and Native Americans.

instinctively how to entertain, adding enough plot twists and romance to keep readers turning page after page. She set her stories in places she could describe in intimate detail: the Limberlost Swamp, the Wabash River valley, and the woodlands near Sylvan Lake. Likewise, she created fictional characters based on real people she knew. "I live in the country and work in the woods," she once explained, "so no other location is possible for my backgrounds, and only the people with whom I come in daily contact there are suitable for my actors." Beyond that, she appealed to readers by preaching traditional values. Her characters suffered hardships and faced obstacles. But through hard work, determination, and decency—as well as close contact with nature— they overcame their problems and experienced "wholeness."

The reading public understood that her novels were "escapist" entertainment. Yet in the early 1900s, as the country itself was undergoing dramatic change, escapism was precisely what many readers wanted. Since the Civil War, Americans had begun leaving family farms and moving to cities in record numbers. The nation's agricultural economy had rapidly given way to factory jobs sparked by the expansion of railroads and the emerging steel and oil industries.

Joining farm folk and villagers in the growing cities were waves of immigrants. Between 1870 and 1900, the nation's population doubled, exceeding seventy-six million. Two decades later, the shift from rural to urban life became even more pronounced. By 1920 more Americans lived in cities and towns than on farms or in villages of less than twenty-five thousand.

The loss of rural life left many Americans feeling nostalgic. Many longed for a return to a simpler, more neighborly, less stressful time. As wildlife and wild places were destroyed to make way for industry, many Americans also grew wistful for pastoral environments. Thus, Stratton-Porter's novels appealed to readers on two levels. She honored, through her fictional heroes and heroines, the old-fashioned virtues that many Americans struggled to cling to. She also led them to a place where many had never been or where they wanted to return—to flowering meadows and clean-smelling woods and marshes alive with birdsong.

Readers were most receptive to Stratton-Porter's stories in the years leading up to and including World War I. By 1915 her books were selling at such a staggering rate that someone estimated they would, if piled one atop another, be sixteen hundred times higher than the world's tallest building. The war years brought Stratton-Porter new followers. Battle-weary American soldiers, sick of the mud, dying, and destruction they were witnessing in France, carried inexpensive reprints of *Freckles* and *A Girl of the Limberlost* into the trenches with them. "I shall now . . . imagine I am in the swamps of Indiana," an army chaplain wrote her after picking up a copy of *A Girl of the Limberlost*. A few days later, he wrote her again: "I was astonished when I finished the book to see that it was 2 a.m. I surely enjoyed it. It sounded so American, and the Nature suggestions brought me back to myself again."

Just as Americans embraced her novels, so did readers around the world. From London, England, a businessman sent word that "your books are among my valued possessions." From Peking, China, an English teacher wrote that her books were a "blessing." A professor's wife wanted Stratton-Porter to know "what pleasure and profit your works are to many in Africa." And an Australian schoolgirl shared that she and her friends had organized a "Gene Stratton-Porter Night" to discuss their favorite characters. Her books eventually were published in fourteen different languages—from Arabic to Czech to Norwegian. In 1917 a British military officer addressed her fame this way: "I am writing this chiefly to thank you for the grand work you have done for humanity. I have travelled in India, Afghanistan, Cashmir, the Straits

Settlements, China, Japan, Java, round Australia, and I have seen how your work is honoured all over the earth."

Literary critics, meanwhile, picked apart Stratton-Porter's fiction. Unable to accept her "sugary" vision of life, many openly scorned her work. "She is mistress of a recipe of cuteness, triteness, and sentimentality," sniffed a critic for *The Nation*. Prominent editor Frederic Taber Cooper grumbled that her characters acted "half way between melodrama and a grown-up fairy tale." Even a minister complained that her novels were nothing but "molasses fiction." But to all who faulted her work, Stratton-Porter had an answer: "Now what do I care for the newspaper or magazine critic yammering that . . . my pictures of life are sentimental and idealized. They are! And I glory in them!" She especially rejected modern writers such as Hoosier novelist Theodore Dreiser whose fiction was raw and gloomy. "To my way of thinking . . . the greatest service a piece of fiction can do any reader," Stratton-Porter argued, "is to leave him with a higher ideal of life than he had when he began. If in one small degree it shows him where he can be a gentler, saner, cleaner, kindlier man, it is a wonder-working book."

Critics also dismissed Stratton-Porter's nature books, insisting her work was not scientific enough. She admittedly was not a trained scientist; she quit high school just shy of graduation. Her popularity as a novelist likely also hurt her standing among scholars. She was seen as writing for the masses, rather than the learned. Still, readers appreciated what the critics did not: Stratton-Porter wrote about wildlife in a way that people could understand, without the dry statistics, incomprehensible jargon, and unpronounceable scientific words.

Despite her lack of formal education, Stratton-Porter carefully read the works of respected naturalists, including Thoreau, Muir, and

Above: A Stratton-Porter photograph of two young wood robins. **Left:** Stratton-Porter at work in the field in California, circa 1924.

Burroughs. She also studied the writings of the entomologist Jean-Henri Fabre, who published ten volumes on insects. But instead of mimicking their field methods or copying their writing style, she relied on her sharp-eyed skills as an observer and her accuracy as a reporter to inform readers about outdoor life. Her bird photographs, painstakingly filmed, gave added credibility to her nature studies. After reading her *Homing with the Birds* (1919), the writer Christopher Morley commented: "It is a book to be proud of. . . . I cannot see that Mrs. Porter's great work with birds is any inferior to the studies of the famous Fabre with insects."

A self-taught photographer, Stratton-Porter acquired her first camera in 1895 as a Christmas present from her husband and daughter. By then, the importance of photography to dramatize issues and record physical beauty had become increasingly clear. Photographs of the Yellowstone area by William H. Jackson, one of America's earliest photographers, helped persuade Congress to make that wilderness a national park. Impressed with her own backyard wilderness, Stratton-Porter wanted to visually record the Limberlost's beauty, starting with the colorful array of birds.

Photographs of North American birds and animals were not rare in the late 1800s. But the subjects typically were dead and stuffed. Stratton-Porter would have none of that. Determined to get photos of live birds in their natural habitat, she hauled her box cameras, tripod, and glass plates deep into the wild and set up the equipment wherever she found nests. With patience and discipline, she waited hours until the birds behaved naturally, paying no attention to her or the camera. She waited, too, for the best sunlight and shadow. The results were close-up photographs that, as one later writer put it, "startle because of their lifelike quality." And as Stratton-Porter proudly noted, the photographs were secured without injuring or killing birds. Her pioneering work in the field helped set the standard for nature photographers who followed her.

Though she remained vigorous into her sixties, Stratton-Porter's life ended abruptly on December 6, 1924, in a car accident near her Los Angeles home. Legions of her fans mourned, and newspapers across the country carried her obituary. In the Adirondack Forest Preserve in New York, a forest of white pines was dedicated to her. The American Reforestation Association likewise honored her conservation work by planting "memorial" trees in each Los Angeles schoolyard.

Always fiercely proud, Stratton-Porter hoped that the literary critics who harshly judged her writing would eventually be proven wrong. "Time, the hearts of my readers, and the files of my publishers will find me my ultimate place," she once said. Whatever her "ultimate" place, she was a writer to be reckoned with in her day. Her bibliographer David MacLean noted that between 1895 and 1945, only fifty-five books had racked up American sales of one million or more copies. She wrote five of them, outdistancing even such heralded names as Mark Twain and Rudyard Kipling. Her readership, at its peak, was estimated at fifty million and her earnings from her literary activities were estimated at two million dollars.

Today, Stratton-Porter is remembered for her drive and her daring. At a time when women were supposed to concern themselves solely with their families and homes, she pushed back society's boundaries, developed her talents, pursued her interests, and willed herself to succeed. Passionate about nature, she committed herself to persuading people to get up off sofas, explore the outdoors, and investigate nature's

Although birds were her first love, Stratton-Porter became entranced by moths.

wonders. As a photographer, her name lives on, too. Her detailed depictions of bird life reveal a vitality and immediacy that make her nature photographs timeless.

Perhaps her lasting legacy is that she issued environmental wake-up calls long before it was fashionable to do so. Stratton-Porter was an early and vocal advocate for preserving wildlife, streams, and woodlands, and her advocacy extended far beyond her Limberlost territory. One of her last written pleas was to save the elk of Jackson Hole, Wyoming, near Yellowstone National Park. She also foresaw global warming and understood then what the science now shows— that the wanton cutting down of trees can affect changes in local climate. Forcefully, she argued that people must be aware of the profound damage they can do to the natural world. Repeatedly, she urged Americans to preserve the environment for future generations.

At Stratton-Porter's death, the Izaak Walton League, a national conservation organization, called on its members to "carry on in the cause for which she worked and in which she believed with every atom of her heart and soul." And in what was perhaps the most fitting tribute to this Hoosier-born nature lover, the league, in its monthly publication *Outdoor America*, declared: "If we can dedicate to her memory something of the unspoiled forests of her dreams, we shall have erected the monument she would have chosen; if we can write her epitaph in terms of clean rivers, clean outdoor playgrounds, and clean young hearts, we shall have done what she would have asked."

1

In the summer of 1863 Americans braced themselves for death and dying. The Civil War had entered its third year, and the bloodbath showed no signs of ending. In July more than 160,000 Union and Confederate soldiers clashed outside the little town of Gettysburg, Pennsylvania, in the bloodiest battle in American history. An estimated fifty thousand men were killed, wounded, captured, or missing. Amid so much suffering and sorrow that painful summer, an aging couple in Indiana awaited happier news. On August 17, Mark and Mary Stratton's twelfth child, a healthy daughter, was born. They named her Geneva Grace.

She would be their last child. By then, Mark was fifty years old and Mary forty-seven. Full of the pioneer spirit, Mark had moved to the Indiana wilderness from Ohio more than two decades earlier, in 1838. He bought land, cleared trees, and set rail fences on 160 acres in upper Wabash County on the border with Kosciusko County. After establishing one farm, he moved south and carved out another farmstead near the Wabash County settlement of Lagro, a village near the new Wabash and Erie Canal, built to help farmers ship their grain and pork to distant markets. There, the ambitious and business-savvy Mark began to prosper financially. By the time daughter Geneva arrived, he supported his family comfortably.

Geneva (who later shortened her name to Gene) loved the family farm. It sat on 240 acres of rolling land, crossed by three streams. The white, two-story farmhouse was a picture of order and tidiness. A white picket fence ran across the front yard. Nearby was a red barn with a big yard for animals, smaller houses for chickens and ducks, a vegetable garden, and an orchard fragrant with the blossoms of apple, peach, and pear trees. The property went by the name Hopewell Farm. As Gene wrote years later, "No other farm was ever quite so lovely."

Mary's "flower magic" contributed to the farm's beauty. Gene's mother was a small woman, who Mark described as a "ninety-pound bit of pink porcelain, pink as a wild rose, plump as a partridge." But however small Mary's fingers, they could make things grow. Gene remembered how her mother "worked her especial magic with bulbs" and how Hopewell Farm bloomed with colorful tulips, daffodils, lilies,

Mary Stratton   Mark Stratton

dahlias, and hyacinths. "At this she was wonderful," Gene said of her mother's skill with plants. "She started dainty little vines and climbing plants from tiny seeds she found in rice and coffee. . . . She even started trees and shrubs from cuttings no one else would have thought of trying to cultivate."

Mary's lessons in seed sprouting and plant lore took root in her youngest daughter. Whenever Gene saw wildflowers being destroyed by plowing and spading on the farm, she transplanted them to fence corners and other sheltered locations, as well as to her own garden under a huge pear tree. "And this was how," Gene later wrote, "I got my first lesson in conservation."

On this busy working farm, all the Stratton children performed chores. As a toddler, Gene carried woodchips to the fireplace and picked up clothespins that fell to the grass. As a young girl, she fed the chickens, gathered eggs, and pounded bricks into dust to clean knives. Growing older, she shelled corn, sharpened shovels, collected maple syrup, and melted lead for molding bullets. Her training in housekeeping was delayed, however, when her mother became ill. Mary contracted typhoid fever early in Gene's childhood and never fully recovered. With Mary requiring constant bed rest, Gene's older sisters had enough to do without supervising their little sister. Guided by her curiosity, Gene roamed at will outdoors.

Often, she followed her older brothers as they plowed, hunting for Indian arrowheads in the freshly turned dirt. She also gathered ears of corn and made them into dolls, collected goose quills in the barnyard, and napped in fence corners. As long as she showed up promptly at mealtimes, her family asked few questions. "By the day," Gene recalled, "I trotted from one object which attracted me to another, singing a little song of made-up phrases about everything I saw while I waded

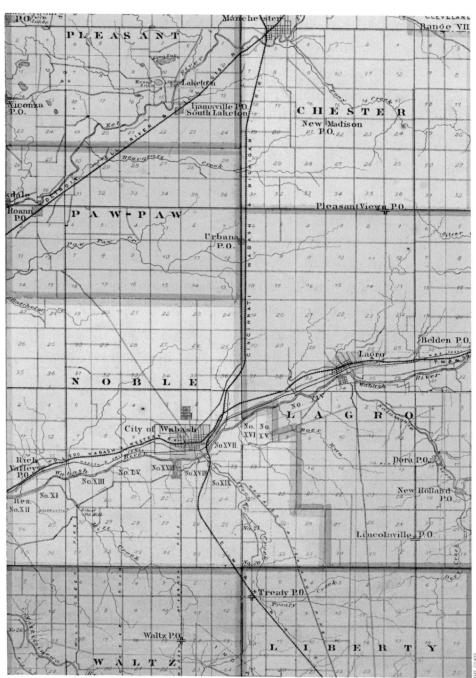

An 1875 map of Wabash County. Lagro is located just northeast of Wabash in
Lagro Township.

catching fish, chasing butterflies over clover fields, or following a bird with a hair in its beak." On her wanderings, she followed her father's example of respecting wildlife. Before long, she was befriending wild creatures, too. She made pets of baby squirrels and rabbits, fed sweetened water to butterflies, and nursed wounded animals back to health.

Watching birds was among her favorite pastimes. Gene loved sitting in the forked branch of a catalpa tree near the front gate, scanning the sky for larks, cardinals, passenger pigeons, and swallows. Occasionally, she glimpsed red-tailed hawks up among the clouds, and she marveled at their freedom: "I envied these birds their power to soar in the face of the wind, to ride with the stiff gale of a beating storm, or to hang motionless as if frozen in air, according to their will, as I envied nothing else on earth."

Mark observed his daughter's keen interest in birdlife. His own love of winged creatures led him to teach her they were a gift from God.

The Stratton home at Hopewell Farm, located north of the village of Lagro.

Gene saw that birds added beauty to the world through their songs and colorful presence. Her father explained how they also helped protect the farm's fruit and crops by eating insects. He did not just instruct with words. One of Gene's early memories was of her father lifting her to look into a hummingbird nest, where she spotted two tiny eggs. Before raising her up, Mark tied a handkerchief over her mouth, a lesson in how wild creatures must be approached in quiet.

As Gene's fascination with birds grew, Mark declared that all birds on the farm belonged to her, and she was to protect them. Thrilled with her new assignment, Gene spent an entire spring locating sixty-four nests. She chased away cats and snakes, and when the young hatched, she fed them daily from the pocket of her apron—bits of hard-boiled egg, boiled potato, grain, caterpillars, and worms. She first observed what the mother birds fed their young, noting those that ate seeds and those that ate meat.

Accustomed to Gene tiptoeing around their nests, the adult birds did not seem to mind her visits. "I was the friend and devoted champion of every bird that nested in the garden, on the fences, on the ground, in the bushes, in the dooryard, or in the orchard trees," she recalled years later. "From breakfast until dinner and from dinner until supper, almost my entire day was spent in making the rounds of these nests, watching the birds while they built, brooded, or fed their young."

Before long, a blue jay became her pet, sitting on her shoulder as she worked and played. She named the bird Hezekiah and dressed it in pants, a coat, and a sunbonnet. She even taught it a trick—to roll cherries across the floor before eating them. Other favorite playmates were a brown thrasher named Peter and a bantam rooster named Bobby. Gene taught Bobby to crow at the mention of the word "Amen!" But even as she had favorites, she loved all the birds on the

Gene at the age of ten, shortly before moving from her beloved Hopewell Farm to the city of Wabash.

farm, from the little brown wren that sang from the top of the pump to the green warbler nesting in wild sweetbriar beside the back porch. Her devotion to birds led her mother to call her "a little bird woman."

When winter approached and her beloved birds flew south, Gene found other amusements on the farm. Outdoors, in the snow, she sledded down a hill next to the orchard. Indoors, she curled in her father's lap after dinner. "He was constantly reading aloud to us children and to visitors, descriptions of the great deeds of men," Gene recalled. Mark was known for delivering his readings with gusto, especially on the subject of English history. He displayed equal flair when reciting chapters of the Bible. His biblical knowledge helped him pass an exam to become a licensed Methodist preacher. On a corner of his farm, Mark donated land and helped build a church, where he conducted services on Sundays.

To Gene, her father's gift for storytelling and dramatic expression counted among his many admirable qualities. "He had a streak of genius in his make-up: the genius of large appreciation," she wrote years later. "Over inspired Biblical passages, over great books, over sunlit landscapes, over a white violet abloom in deep shade, over a heroic deed of man, I have seen his brow light up, his eyes shine."

Gene's first schoolhouse was the family farmhouse. Her brother, Irvin, on leave from college due to an accident, taught his little sister her ABCs one summer. Other family members pitched in as instructors. "I had been drilled at home and I could understand any ordinary printed matter and spell quite well before I ever started to school," she recalled. "My first literary effort was printed in wobbly letters in the back of an old grammar. It was entitled 'Ode to the Moon,' not that I had any idea what an 'ode' was other than that I had heard it discussed in the family, together with epic and sonnet, as forms of poetic expression."

When she was old enough to attend the Lagro Township school, a stubborn Gene refused to go. For the first month her sister, Ada, had to coax and tug the crying child to class. Gene hated that she had to sit indoors when scented woods and berry patches and clover fields beckoned. She also hated wearing uncomfortable clothes, long stockings, and heavy shoes. Saturday evenings were bad enough. That's when Gene's heavy brown hair that hung in braids had to be washed and curled for the next day's church services. Now school meant similar torture—in terms of dress and being cooped up.

To make matters worse, Gene especially disliked the township teacher. One day the teacher wrote on the blackboard: "Little birds in their nests agree." Gene, excited to encounter a familiar subject, spoke up. "Oh, but they *don't* agree! They fight like everything! They pull feathers and peck at each other's eyes until they are all bloody!" The teacher did not like being contradicted. Gene was punished for being disrespectful.

Even when the school day was over, lessons continued at home. Mark drilled his children in spelling and defining words from a McGuffey reader, a commonly used schoolbook. He also insisted they write on their slates in preparation for the next day's lessons. In her father's presence, Gene became a dutiful student. Mark, in turn, ramped up his instruction. "When we became so expert . . . that it became tiresome," Gene recalled, "he branched out into geography and readers for broader culturing."

When Gene was eight years old, her sister, Mary Ann, by then married and living away from home, died from injuries in a railway accident. Five months later, in July 1872, her teenage brother, Leander, drowned while swimming in the Wabash River. Of all her siblings, Gene most adored Leander, whom she called Laddie. He was kind, dependable, and thoughtful, always ready to answer her questions. As the oldest brother still at home, he helped raised Gene and together they shared a deep love of the farm. When his body was carried home from the river that July day, Gene ran screaming to her mother, clutching Laddie's boots in her hands. Family members tried to console her, but they too were grief stricken. Years later, Gene's daughter, Jeannette Porter Meehan, wrote: "Laddie's death . . . left an ache for ever in the heart of his Little Sister."

The drowning forced Mark to make some hard decisions. He worried about his wife, whose health grew noticeably worse after losing two children in such a short time. He also worried about the future of the farm. Then sixty years old, Mark had leaned on Laddie to manage the property and intended to turn it over to him. After weighing various options, Mark eventually decided that the family would be better off if he retired and leased the farm. In the fall of 1874 he arranged for himself, his wife, and four children—Gene included—to move in with Anastasia Taylor, another of Gene's married sisters. Gene protested loudly. Anastasia lived ten miles away in the town of Wabash, and town life meant Gene would have to give up her birds.

When moving day arrived, Gene remained defiant. She refused to board the carriage for Wabash. Her father, knowing his eleven-year-old daughter to be as strong-willed as himself, finally bowed to one of her demands. In return for Gene saying good-bye to the farm and all the wildlife she loved, she was permitted to take with her *nine* pet birds.

2

Wabash, Indiana, was a bustling community of four thousand
people in 1874. Along with being the seat of government for Wabash
County, the city boasted a sound school system over which Gene
Stratton's brother, Irvin, had recently been appointed as superintendent.
The city also had the advantage of two railroads, both sparking
economic development, as had the Wabash and Erie Canal decades
earlier. New and expanding industries were turning out everything
from buggies to furniture to cigars. Downtown merchants shared in
the prosperity, stocking rakes, wallpaper, shawls, and candy—most
anything townsfolk or farmers needed.

Gene Stratton's sister, Anastasia, and her lawyer husband, Alvah
Taylor, lived near the railroad tracks on a busy and dusty street.
There, the clicking of rails and rumble of freight trains replaced
woodland sounds that Gene had grown accustomed to. Clean air was
scarce, too. Soot from burning coal at nearby factories drifted and
settled everywhere, darkening even the courthouse. Foul odors also
were an ever-present problem. Manure piles littered alleys and the
slaughterhouse added its own stench.

It was in this new environment, and into the Taylor home, that
Gene and her pet birds settled. She had barely unpacked, however,
when family life was upended again. In February 1875, only four

months after moving to Wabash, Mary Stratton died. In the span of three years, Gene had lost a sister, a brother, and her mother. The family buried Mary in a cemetery on Hopewell Farm. Fittingly, her grave was near a cedar tree Mary had planted years earlier from cuttings she had carried from Ohio. In Mary's capable hands, the cuttings grew into two immense trees, especially the one near her burial spot. Recalling her mother years later, Gene wrote: "To me her real monument is a cedar. . . . that tree must stand thirty feet tall now, and have a body two feet in circumference."

As she mourned the loss of her mother, Gene resented a new reality. In Wabash she was expected to attend school eight months a year. She still disliked the classroom and hated how teachers never "made the slightest effort to discover what I cared for personally, what I had been born to do." Their only goal, as she saw it, was to push her "into the groove in which all other pupils ran." Gene also felt uneasy around her new classmates. A former student, recalling Gene's first days

Above: A view of Wabash Street, south from Market Street, in Wabash, Indiana, circa 1900s. **Opposite:** The Wabash County Courthouse in Wabash.

Gene at age sixteen. During her teenage years, she developed a taste for music by such famous composers as Franz Schubert, Richard Wagner, Franz Liszt, and Wolfgang Amadeus Mozart.

at school, remembered her as being a "perfect example of rugged health. . . . her bright brown hair hung in two heavy braids; she wore a gay plaid dress and a white bib apron."

It was Gene's appearance—her plain manner of dress and her lack of hair ribbons—that contributed to her unease. She saw herself as too much the "farm girl" and began to wish that she, too, could buy niceties. "I had been trained from the day of my birth that I must not ask for things," she recalled. "I must be content with what was provided for me. And I was *not* content. I wanted dresses such as Edith Elliot wore, and hair ribbons like Madge Busick's. I wanted a carriage like the McCray [McCrea] girls', and trips to Florida like the Gillen girls'."

To take her mind off money she did not have, Gene continued caring for her pet birds. She scraped perches, changed sand, and made the cages shine. By the time she entered Wabash High School, she also looked for ways to improve herself. Her sister, Florence, gave her banjo, violin, and piano lessons, and Gene dutifully practiced for hours every day. Upon observing other girls learning how to paint on china and canvas, Gene asked her father for lessons. Mark Stratton, though strapped for cash, agreed. He paid the teacher with potatoes and apples from his rented farm. Florence, meanwhile, did her best to help Gene appear more fashionable. Florence gave music lessons to the children of a local dressmaker, who in turn provided Gene with more stylish clothes.

Even as she worked to win social acceptance, Gene retained her independent thinking. If a subject interested her, she made passing grades in school. If it failed to attract her attention, she refused to do the work. Years later she shared a story about her high school teacher assigning her to write a paper on "Mathematical Law." Gene hated mathematics, and she was convinced the teacher, in selecting that topic, purposely wished to punish her. Angry, she put off doing the assignment as long as possible. The night before it was due she announced to herself: "I can't do a paper on Mathematics, and I won't!"

Instead, she reviewed *Picciola*, a book by the French author Xavier Boniface Saintine. Gene dearly loved the book, a prized volume in the Stratton family library. *Picciola* is about a jailed Italian nobleman who, deprived of his freedom and possessions, finds joy in a little green sprout that blossoms among the cobblestones in the prison yard. Gene felt a special kinship to the nobleman. As she put it, "He got into political trouble . . . and I had got into mathematical trouble."

Gene also loved the story because she understood birds and flowers—how a bird flying over the prison yard likely dropped the seed that sprouted and grew into the "thirty perfect blossoms." Wasting no time, Gene picked up her pencil that evening and poured out the tale. "Breathlessly I wrote for hours. I exceeded the [page] limit ten times over," she recalled. "Saintine's masterpiece . . . was one of the things I knew more about than any teacher could teach me."

The next day, Gene read her paper aloud at school, as required. But soon after she began, her instructor ordered her to stop. The superintendent was summoned. Gene was told to begin again, and soon she observed that her listeners were totally absorbed, laughing one minute, crying the next. Tears even ran down the superintendent's cheeks. "My paper was good," she wrote of that memorable day. "It was as good as I had believed it. It was better than I had known."

Sensing a newfound talent, Gene began to write in earnest. She hid behind her books at school and wrote. When she should have been studying at home, she wrote. Her grades fell lower and lower, but still she neglected her studies. "When I was supposed to be laboring over Greek and geometry, I wrote a book of poetry, two books of fiction, and many stories, all of which I destroyed later, and now fervently wish that I had not," she noted. Gene especially fancied herself as a poet: "I cannot remember the time when I was not interested in poetry and trying to write it."

Gene's frustration with classwork apparently reached a breaking point in the spring of 1883, her final year of high school. Consulting no one, she quit school. Her decision came during a stressful time for the Stratton family. Anastasia, who had been ill with cancer for more than a year, was away receiving treatment at an Illinois medical clinic. She died in April. Mark, who had moved with daughters Gene and Ada to a house down the street, decided they should move back into the Taylor home to help Alvah and the couple's two children.

Amid all this upheaval, Gene no longer had her birds to amuse or comfort her. Her failing grades had led Mark to issue an order: the birds had to go and the cages were to be stored. In later years, Gene shared little information about that difficult spring or her decision to leave school. But she insisted she had no regrets: "I studied harder after leaving school than ever before, and in a manner that did me real good. . . . The best that can be said of what education I have is that it was strictly private. . . . I studied the things in which I was most interested."

The winter of 1883 proved to be equally difficult for Gene. In December she caught her foot in a sidewalk grate and fell, knocking herself unconscious and cracking her skull. As Gene's daughter, Jeannette Porter Meehan, later recounted, her family "despaired of saving her," and Gene was forced to spend several weeks in bed. When she could finally move about, she needed a cane to walk.

By summer, however, Gene had greatly improved. Ready for a change of scenery and some fun, she accepted an invitation to stay with friends at their cottage on Sylvan Lake near Rome City, about seventy miles north of Wabash. The lake was a popular vacation spot. People flocked to a large wooded island in the middle of the lake to attend a Chautauqua—a program that combined adult education, recreation, entertainment, and, often, religious instruction. The name came from Chautauqua Lake in western New York, where a summer program for Sunday-school teachers started in 1874.

Gene had attended her first Chautauqua at Sylvan Lake three years earlier. Joining her then were her sisters, Florence and Ada. Gene enjoyed the lectures, concerts, and songfests. But the lakeside resort's biggest appeal was that it offered her an escape from city life. She was back among wild birds and breathing fresh air. Her hosts, on her return visit, were the Reverend and Mrs. C. H. Wilkinson. Their daughter, Cora, was Gene's age, and together the girls explored the lake by rowboat while fishing for black bass and paddling towards shorelines

Cabins and docks line the shoreline of Sylvan Lake in Rome City, Indiana.

Charles Dorwin Porter

to gather white water lilies. Ashore, they picnicked and picked wild berries. The days were long and lazy, and Gene, still not wholly recovered from her fall, felt revived.

It was on that visit, in the summer of 1884, that Gene made the mistake of offering a straw full of raspberries to another young woman. Gene did so in friendship. But the offer was rejected, and Gene was scorned for behaving "unladylike." Gene had already observed that other vacationing women did not share her zest for the water and woods. She also understood that "ladies" of her generation much preferred to embroider, paint, or daintily fan themselves in the family parlor than to tramp in thick woods, risk bug bites and dirt, and allow their faces to become suntanned. Gene had no desire to be like them. Gradually, she saw she might even be of some service to them: "I came in time to believe that there might be a lifework for one woman in leading these other women back to the forest." Referencing the Bible, she added: "On account of my inclinations, education and rearing I felt in a degree equipped to be their Moses."

Not yet twenty-one, Gene was not yet equipped to lead anyone anywhere. She did, however, have a follower that summer, of which she was unaware. As she limped around the resort, a thirty-four-year-old drugstore owner watched her with interest. His name was Charles Dorwin Porter. A bachelor, he wished to meet the handsome young woman, with the clear gray eyes, thick eyebrows, and dark brown hair. He dared not casually approach her, however. Etiquette of the day required formal introductions. So Charles spoke to his cousin, who spoke to a relative of Gene's, and he eventually learned of her name and address. Charles vowed to write her a letter. Two months later, he did.

3

If Charles Porter needed courage to write Gene Stratton, he found a dose of it in mid-September of 1884. By then he had returned to work at his drugstore in Geneva, a hamlet in Adams County. The town sat near the Wabash River, forty miles upstream from where Gene was born. Charles began his letter by saying he had been "rather favourably impressed" with Gene's appearance and was venturing "the forwardness to address" her. He introduced himself and his business affairs and then politely asked her to reply: "May I hope to have a line from you? or do you think I have overreached all bounds of propriety?"

Other women might have proceeded more cautiously. Charles was, as Gene herself noted, "an entire stranger." But she refused to be bound by rigid rules and conventions. Instead, she promptly penned a reply, telling him about herself and her family and stating she would like to hear from him again. A correspondence ensued, with the two regularly exchanging letters. Always addressing Charles as "Mr. Porter," Gene did not hold back her opinions. In an early letter, she made clear that "I think differently from most people; so prepare to be shocked." She also offered confessions: "I made some cookies *and they were not fit to eat!*" and "I don't *like* housekeeping by any means, but if I *have* to do it I mean to march it through."

A photograph of Gene Stratton-Porter shortly after her marriage in 1886.

Ten months passed before the couple finally met. When the following summer rolled around, Gene again vacationed at Sylvan Lake, and Charles traveled there to openly court her. On Gene's return to Wabash, their letter writing resumed, with marriage surfacing as a topic. Gene informed Charles she was no "howler for woman's rights." But she also insisted married men expected too much of their wives. In a letter dated September 1885, Gene asked how any woman could be "bright and cheerful" when a husband would "lay on a girl's shoulders the management and planning of a house, then . . . have her cook, wash, bake, iron, scrub, make beds, sweep, and dust." Such feistiness and honesty failed to scare off Charles. A month later, the two were engaged to be married.

The wedding took place the following spring, on April 21, 1886, in sister Ada's Wabash home. By then, Gene had completed the shortening of her first name. Born Geneva, she had abbreviated it to "Geneve" during her school days in Wabash. When corresponding with Charles, she had further shortened her name to "Gene," apparently because he liked the simpler form. When they married, Gene took Charles's surname. But exercising her usual independence, she also retained her maiden name and added a hyphen, the result being Gene Stratton-Porter. Charles sometimes affectionately called his wife "Genie;" others frequently addressed her as "Mrs. Porter." She continued to address Charles as "Mr. Porter." Later, in her nonfiction work, she called him by another name as well—"The Deacon."

Charles selected the town of Decatur for the couple's first home. The county-seat community was midway between Geneva and Fort Wayne, where Charles operated a second drugstore. He had grown up in Decatur, and shortly before the wedding, he bought back the old Porter family homestead. His mother had died eighteen months

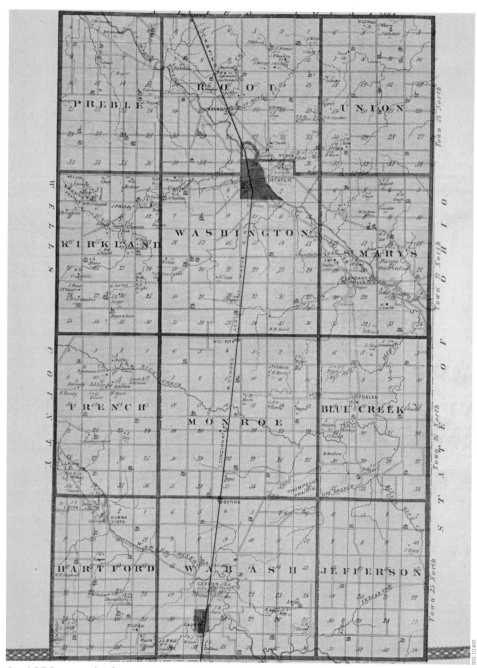

An 1876 map of Adams County, Indiana. Geneva is located at the bottom, middle, of the map, in Wabash Township.

earlier, and his father, a physician in the Union army, was killed in 1864 during the Civil War. Charles assumed his new bride would be happy in the two-story frame house on Main Street. He even offered to enlarge it. Having spent the last ten years of her life boarding with relatives, Stratton-Porter at first thought she would be happy there. After all, it was a home of her *own*. But the house was dark and cramped, with no backyard for flowers or shrubs. And Decatur appealed to her no more than Wabash had. Worse, Charles often worked late and missed the train home from Geneva, leaving her to pass long days alone.

By the fall, Stratton-Porter was itching to move. Her brother, Irvin, announced in September 1886 that he was packing up and heading to Kansas to become a cattleman. Kansas failed to excite her interest, but

Stratton-Porter at age twenty-five.

the Black Hills of Dakota did. The discovery of gold there in 1874 had prompted white settlers to pour into the region. Eager for adventure, Stratton-Porter wrote to Charles at his work: "I've thought until I nearly split my head. I can see but one way for us and that is to go to Dakota and take a claim . . . and live *out* a year or two. It won't hurt us, and then, if you have the drug fever, we'll go to town and get you a store."

But her "Dakota fever" did not last. Stratton-Porter learned she was expecting a baby, and in

August 1887 the couple's only child, a daughter, was born. She was named Jeannette, after Charles's sister. At his wife's insistent urging, Charles finally agreed to buy a house in Geneva, where he could walk to his business (he had earlier sold his interests in the Fort Wayne drugstore). The following spring, the three of them settled into a yellow cottage within a few blocks of the Geneva drugstore. The yard had an orchard, a chicken house, and a barn for the horse and buggy. Stratton-Porter was content. She grew even more so upon resuming an old hobby: collecting pet birds.

Her collection began with a green linnet. She found him a mate, and soon there were more than a dozen youngsters under a green-roofed cage. "When the birds of this cage were asleep in a row, filling the highest perch, with their heads tucked under their wings, and their feathers fluffed in cold weather, they looked exactly like gaudy swan's down powder puffs," she recalled. To her delight, a relative brought her

Charles Dorwin Porter loved to fish, as did Gene.

a black-headed grosbeak from Mexico. Another relative, sister Florence, sent her a parrot named Major. To this collection, Stratton-Porter added two half-starved cardinals and a pair of oriole nestlings.

Along with caring for Jeannette and her bevy of birds, Stratton-Porter continued to indulge her love of music. She worked at perfecting her piano skills and took violin lessons from a teacher who traveled from a neighboring town. She also took classes in embroidery and china painting. Eventually, she even organized a women's club to study literature. Stratton-Porter wrote a paper for the group in which she interpreted *Leaves of Grass* by the American poet Walt Whitman. Whitman's work was not yet widely appreciated in the United States, at least not to the extent that it was acclaimed in Europe. But Stratton-Porter loved *Leaves of Grass* for its unconventional form, pulsing rhythms, and celebration of nature. "If you love the green grass, flowers, and trees: if you know what the leaves whisper and the waters murmur and the birds sing; if you love God's creation above man's manufacturing—read the book," she urged her clubwomen. "You will be better for it."

Charles's fortunes, meanwhile, continued to improve in the little village of Geneva. Oil had recently been discovered in the area, and Charles, who owned acres of farmland in Adams County, soon earned a steady income from sixty oil wells drilled on his property. The discovery of all this "black gold," as the oil was called, brought swarms of newcomers to town. A bank was needed, and Charles, who housed a large vaultlike safe in his drugstore, sensed an opportunity. In 1892 he started the Geneva Bank. By the following year, the thrifty Charles believed he had saved enough money to treat Gene to a vacation. In the fall of 1893, the couple traveled to Chicago to see the World's Columbian Exposition.

The fair was staged to honor Columbus's arrival in America four hundred years earlier. Set in a park on the shores of Lake Michigan, the fair attracted nearly twenty-six million Americans, all eager to see the many pools, canals, and fountains, not to mention the cavernous buildings. Stratton-Porter especially liked the huge Forestry Building. Tree trunks, of the finest timber and each twenty-five feet high, served as porch columns on all sides. Stratton-Porter had begun to feel cramped in her "little yeller house." She left Chicago dreaming of a large rustic home, inspired by what she had just seen.

With Charles's blessing, she began working with an architect. She helped design a two-story house on an open lot near the yellow cottage. Construction began in the spring of 1894, and the new dwelling, like the Forestry Building in Chicago, featured wood, inside and out. Wisconsin cedar logs were used to build the lower level. Redwood

Crowds line up to visit the Manufacturer's Building at the World's Columbian Exposition in Chicago.

shingles covered the upper story and roof. A colonnaded porch ran along two sides. Indoors, floors were white oak, walls were paneled in quarter-sawn red oak, and much of the furniture was solid mahogany. Owl carvings adorned the headboard of the Porters' walnut bed.

Stratton-Porter called her new home a cabin, but it was clearly a spacious one. The fourteen rooms included a library, music room, and small greenhouse with windows that allowed wild birds to come and go freely. As impressive as the house was (it was one of the most expensive in town), so were the grounds. The property consisted of a cedar-log barn, fruit trees, a vegetable garden, and bushes and flowers planted to attract birds and insects.

The new home took a year to complete. The couple had barely settled in when, as daughter Jeannette later put it, her mother's "executive ability was put to a severe test." In June 1895 a fire broke out

Men gather around a gushing oil well in Adams County, circa 1900.

late one night in Geneva's business district. Charles was out of town. Awakened by shouts and screams, Stratton-Porter pulled a skirt over her nightgown, grabbed a sweater, slid into some slippers and, after telling Jeannette to stay put, bolted out the door.

Arriving at the scene, she saw a roaring fire that soon consumed thirty wood-framed businesses, including Charles's drugstore. The town lacked a fire department, and although many men came running, no one took charge. They seemed powerless to act. Sizing up the situation, Stratton-Porter organized a water brigade, directed men where to go, and ordered women to wrap wet towels around the men's heads for protection. "Her long hair was flying unnoticed; the frail slippers were burned through from stepping on fallen embers, and her feet were bleeding," said Jeannette, who left the cabin and observed with the crowd. She recalled how her mother's hands were blistered:

The business section on Line Street in Geneva, Indiana.

"But her courage never faltered, and for three long hours they fought—and won."

A few days later, the local newspaper commented that Stratton-Porter "would make an energetic chief of the fire department when that needful improvement is added to our village." Stratton-Porter, meanwhile, walked away that night with her share of stories. A favorite was about the agitated hotel cook whom she had ordered to pour water on the hotel's back stairs, which were threatened by flames and up which firefighting volunteers were racing. She returned to find the cook pouring milk on the steps. When she asked why, he said the stove water was boiling hot, so he opted for cold milk from the icebox. "I will never forget how she shrieked with laughter as she told us, while we were helping her bandage the burned and swollen feet," said Jeannette. "But that was characteristic of Mother: no matter what the nerve strain or worry, she could always see the funny side to relieve the tension."

Charles immediately decided to rebuild his drugstore. He also decided to invest more heavily in his bank and to build new "bank" rooms next to the Shamrock Hotel, which he also owned and that survived the fire. Those decisions prompted Stratton-Porter to assess the family's financial situation. Their new home had been costly to build. Charles had also strained the family's cash supply by building a new house on his farm property. Stratton-Porter concluded that she had not "chanced upon a life of affluence." Austerity, even penny-pinching, looked to be in her future. If she wanted extra money to spend, she would need to earn it. So she settled on a course of action and never looked back: "You will either sink or you will swim. I swam—slowly, to be sure, but I never once went entirely under. I took up my pen."

Deciding to write what she knew about, she sent an article about wild birdlife to an outdoor magazine. The editors wanted the piece

LIMBERLOST CABIN GENEVA IND.

Above: Stratton-Porter's fourteen-room Limberlost Cabin in Geneva, Indiana. **Right:** Jeannette poses with the family's parrot, Major, perched on her shoulder.

illustrated and planned to use drawings of mounted birds, stuffed and wired. "It requires no great stretch of the imagination to understand how those pictures repelled me. I was horrified," Stratton-Porter said. Still, the editors insisted, and when she refused to allow such illustrations to accompany her text, her work was rejected. "We were at a standstill," she said.

Major helped solve her problem. The parrot had long been permitted to perch atop a chair at the family dining table and eat scraps of food, usually crackers dipped in coffee. One evening, as the family enjoyed oyster stew, Major fussed until he was given an oyster. He ate it with relish. Surprised and amused, Stratton-Porter exclaimed, "How I wish I had a camera!" Not long afterward—Christmas 1895—she received just such a gift from her daughter and Charles. A proud Jeannette had paid ten dollars for the camera.

The first pictures Stratton-Porter took were of Major. As she developed the negatives, using chemicals from Charles's drugstore, she recognized that the very first photograph "contained almost every defect of a beginner's work." Still, she ran through the house shouting gleefully. As streaky as the image was, "I could see clearly that it was a perfectly natural, correct reproduction of a living bird. I had found my medium! I could illustrate what I wrote myself!"

Convinced that she could master the camera, she ordered chemicals and paper, then set to work. "By spring I could make a technically perfect reproduction of Major or any flower in the conservatory, while I even succeeded in photographing the fish in the aquarium," she recalled. Aiming her camera through window glass, she was equally pleased with her photos of birds perching or feeding on the outdoor sills. As her confidence grew and the weather improved, she prepared to take her camera into the field. More than anything, she wanted to photograph birds in their natural habitat—to secure poses of them brooding, feeding, bathing, and mating.

She did not have to venture far to achieve her goal. Less than a mile from her cabin was a vast wilderness of marshlands, streams, narrow lakes, and unbroken forest—a region teeming with a seemingly endless variety of birds, insects, and plants. The region was known as the Limberlost Swamp. It soon became Stratton-Porter's laboratory and her home away from home.

4

The Limberlost Swamp stretched for miles southwest of Geneva, Indiana. Accounts vary as to how it acquired the name; one popular story claimed that a young man nicknamed "Limber Jim" got lost in the dense interior. Whatever the story, the swamp remained for centuries an uncharted backcountry. Only in the late 1800s did lumbermen begin to build log roads around the border, as they sought to cut the swamp's timber for ship masts and fine furniture.

In the winter, when the swamp was draped with snow and frost, it had what Gene Stratton-Porter called a "lacy exquisite beauty." But from May until October, the Limberlost more closely resembled a jungle, oozing with muck, infested with poisonous snakes, abuzz with swarming mosquitoes, and nearly impenetrable due to towering trees, tangled underbrush, and high stiff grass. As Stratton-Porter wrote years later: "A Limberlost trip at that time was not to be joked about. It had not been shorn, branded, and tamed. There were most excellent reasons why I should not go there. . . . In its physical aspect it was a treacherous swamp and quagmire filled with every plant, animal, and human danger known . . . in the Central States."

Despite the dangers, brilliantly colored birds flashed through the Limberlost's treetops and dined in the murky waters. It was these birds—scarlet tanagers, cedar waxwings, yellowhammers, goldfinches,

Nature photographs taken by Stratton-Porter, including a swamp (opposite), a wood robin (below), and a maidenhair fern (bottom).

red-winged blackbirds, and blue herons—that drew Stratton-Porter afield. And it was these birds, along with carpets of wildflowers and countless moths and butterflies, that led her to stride deeper into the foreboding wilderness. Charles Porter ordered her to stay away, fearing for her safety. But she went anyway. She was determined to live her own life. And the Limberlost was ideal for her nature study and photography.

Charles did not let up, however. To interest his wife in wild birdlife elsewhere, he took her on weekend fishing trips to the Wabash River. Soon the wooded banks of the Wabash vied with the Limberlost in becoming her favorite spot. There, as in the swamp, she filled notebooks with her observations. She saw, for example, that baby

A photograph by Stratton-Porter of a cardinal in its nest.

grosbeaks and finches had to be repeatedly coaxed by parents to learn to fly—quite unlike the baby warblers and thrushes that quickly took to the air. She also noted how some young birds on leaving the nest knew almost immediately how to find food; others, such as robins and larks, had to be repeatedly shown how to forage. Even birds' bathing habits attracted her attention. Young crows, she observed, were punished by other crows to the point of death if they did not bathe properly.

Along with the note taking, she sketched birds—in the Limberlost, along the Wabash River, wherever she could find them. As often as possible, she also recorded their activity through her camera lens. To get the close-up pictures she wanted, she practiced what she did as a child, working to gain the birds' trust. She visited nests every day,

A Stratton-Porter photograph of a pair of kingfishers fishing from a stump in the Wabash River.

always inching closer until the parents became accustomed to her presence. Sometimes, she chased away squirrels or snakes; other times, she left food in the nests. Eventually, she set up her camera, often concealing it behind branches or using stepladders and ropes to sling the camera between trees to draw near to nests. Incredibly patient, she sat and waited, hoping and watching for just the right picture. "I have reproduced birds in moments of fear, anger, in full tide of song, while dressing their plumage, taking a sun bath, courting, feeding their young," she wrote. "The recipe for such studies is: Go slow, know birds and understand them, and remain in the woods until . . . they will be perfectly natural in your presence."

Around the time Stratton-Porter took up photography, the hobby had become easier due to a small, lightweight camera introduced by

Youngsters gather around to view an early Kodak camera developed by George Eastman.

George Eastman—the Kodak. Each Kodak camera contained paper-based film wound on rollers. When finished with the roll, owners could send the camera to processing plants owned by Eastman. There, the film was developed and made into prints. The prints and the camera, loaded with new film, were returned to their owner. The company, which marketed the first camera in 1888, developed the slogan: "You Press the Button, We Do the Rest."

Despite the Kodak's popularity, Stratton-Porter preferred, as did many professional photographers, to take photographs with glass plates that were eight inches by ten inches in size. She believed that the plates gave her sharper, more detailed pictures. On her field trips, she always took along two to three dozen plates and often a wagonload of equipment, including four cameras adapted for different types of outdoor work. The equipment was heavy, weighing as much as a hundred pounds. To complicate matters, the glass plates had to be changed after every picture was taken. Because Stratton-Porter often placed her cameras high into trees, she or an assistant had to repeatedly climb ladders to replace the glass plates. Jeannette recalled: "Mother often wore out two strong men on these expeditions." The cameras, meanwhile, were costly. To pay for one, Stratton-Porter sold some of the family's jewelry.

George Eastman

On the back of this photograph of Jeannette taken by Stratton-Porter she wrote: "Her hands filled with anemones and spring beauties."

Below: A group of field rabbits huddle together. **Middle:** A pair of kingfishers. **Right:** A yellow-billed cuckoo.

Back home in her cabin, Stratton-Porter lacked a proper darkroom in which to develop her pictures. She improvised in her bathroom, stuffing rugs under the cracks of doors and pulling the window shutters tight to block out all light. She also improvised in the kitchen, washing her exposed plates (negatives) and prints on meat and turkey platters in the sink. "These arrangements were extremely inconvenient and uncomfortable," she acknowledged. Still, her pictures turned out well— so well that a manufacturer of photographic print paper heard about her work and sent an official to her home, hoping she might share how she achieved her results. Embarrassed, Stratton-Porter talked about the chemical properties of Indiana water, suggesting that might explain her success. Satisfied, the man left. "I did not subject the gentleman to the shock of showing him that my dark-room was the family bath," Stratton-Porter said.

Jeannette and her friend, Sarah Jane Miller, both age twelve, relax while reading a book in front of the fireplace at the Limberlost Cabin. The rug they are sitting on is yellow angora goat skin.

If her picture-developing methods were a bit unusual, so was life inside the cabin. Newly emerged moths and butterflies flew through the house, feeding on flowers in the conservatory and from little saucers of honey and sweetened water set out for their use. Patches of moth eggs, protected by glasses turned upside down, sat on rugs. Wounded birds perched on furniture. Caterpillars filled boxes, and guinea pigs, at one point, occupied the kitchen. Cocoons could usually be found pinned to lace curtains. "I was accustomed to all sorts of birds and little animals and insects in the house," said Jeannette. "I was taught not to be afraid of anything, and I handled all kinds of worms, butterflies, pinching bugs, and caterpillars without injury to myself or to them."

In addition to the unusual houseguests, Stratton-Porter tended to the regular residents—her many canaries and linnets. She also looked after her conservatory in which three hundred to six hundred

A short-eared owl photographed by Stratton-Porter.

bulbs bloomed every winter. As for household duties such as cooking and washing dishes, it is not clear how much time she allotted those. Charles, at least, ate many meals out. Still, years later, Stratton-Porter declared proudly that she kept the cabin "immaculate" and even managed to make most of her daughter's clothes. Jeannette, reflecting on her childhood, remembered her mother this way: "She managed her household affairs with an efficiency and an eye to time-saving that was a source of never-ending envy among her neighbours, most of whom were older and more experienced women."

However efficient she was indoors, Stratton-Porter always made time for her fieldwork. Before heading out in her little horse-drawn buggy or with her spring wagon, she dressed in a khaki-colored skirt that blended with the trees. She wore knee-high leather hiking boots. She draped mosquito netting over a broad-brimmed hat. From spring through autumn, she worked in all kinds of weather and under the most challenging conditions, braving the glare of the sun, the suffocating heat of steaming river valleys, the rank odors of the swamp, and, in her words, "tramps, vicious domestic animals, and cross dogs." Once, while wading the Wabash River to take some pictures, she caught a chill "which ended in congestion that gave me a ten day fight for my life."

Challenging conditions or not, little escaped Stratton-Porter's eye. As Jeannette recalled: "I have seen her stop the horse, clamber down from the buggy, and straighten a wild flower, broken by some careless foot, put the dirt around it, prop it up with a stick or stone, straighten the petals and leaves carefully, and give it a drink from her thermos bottle."

While she occasionally hired oilmen, farmers, or teenaged boys to help her, especially with setting up tall ladders, Stratton-Porter preferred to work alone. She also tried to shield her activities, aware that the town gossips already had labeled her as odd. "Being so afraid of failure and the inevitable ridicule in a community where I was already severely criticized on account of my ideas of housekeeping, dress, and social customs, I purposely kept everything I did as quiet as possible," noted Stratton-Porter. She spoke more openly to Charles, and sometimes asked him to accompany her afield. That was the case when one day Stratton-Porter learned about an unusual sighting deep in the Limberlost. Lumbermen reported seeing a baby bird, white and soft as a powder puff, in a hollow elm tree. Alongside the bird was a large, pale blue egg with brown speckles. Her curiosity aroused, Stratton-Porter determined that she should go see the nest herself. Certain that he could not stop her, Charles agreed to join her. The two of them set off,

The young, black vulture, Little Chicken, from a photograph by Stratton-Porter.

toting an ax, a hatchet, and two revolvers. Stratton-Porter later wrote
about finding the rare nest, home to a family of black vultures—birds
she had never before seen in Indiana:

> I shielded my camera in my arms. . . . At the well we started on
> foot, Mr. Porter in kneeboots, I in waist-high waders. The time
> was late June; we forced our way between steaming, fetid pools,
> through swarms of gnats, flies, mosquitoes, poisonous insects,
> keeping a sharp watch for rattlesnakes. We sank ankle deep at
> every step, and logs we thought solid broke under us. Our progress
> was a steady succession of prying and pulling each other to the
> surface. Our clothing was wringing wet, and the exposed parts of
> our bodies lumpy with bites and stings. My husband found the
> tree, cleared the opening to the great prostrate log, traversed its
> unspeakable odours for nearly forty feet to its farthest recess, and
> brought the baby and egg to the light in his leaf-lined hat.

Stratton-Porter immediately named the baby "Little Chicken."
Wasting little time, she and Charles began hacking away at vines and
cutting down trees to secure more light for her photographs. The

A bird's nest. Stratton-Porter refused to disturb her animal subjects for the sake
of a photograph. "The greatest brutality ever practiced on brooding birds consists
in cutting down, tearing out and placing nests of helpless young for one's own
convenience," she said.

work left them exhausted; the stench made them nauseous. They could endure the location only by covering their mouths and nostrils with handkerchiefs dipped in disinfectant. After securing several photographs, they packed up for home.

But Stratton-Porter was not finished. Every third day for nearly three months, she and Charles returned to study and photograph Little Chicken. The egg, beautiful as it was, never hatched; the mother broke it and ate the contents. That probably was fortunate. Stratton-Porter's nerves and stamina were pushed to the limit caring for *just* the baby vulture. When Little Chicken's parents grew indifferent about feeding it, she brought it food. She even made arrangements, when she had to leave town for a few days, to bring Little Chicken to her cabin. A hired woman fed the vulture until Stratton-Porter's return, when it was taken back to the swamp. There, with camera lens aimed, Stratton-Porter continued to record Little Chicken's growth.

"This was the beginning of a series of swamp-studies that is, in all probability, without an equal in natural history or photography," she wrote of her long encounter with the vulture. She hastened to add: "There is no way of adequately describing what we endured for that series of pictures."

5

In the late 1800s, fashion-conscious women wore hats trimmed with bird feathers. Sometimes hats featured whole stuffed birds. To satisfy the fashion industry, the slaughter of wild birds grew so rampant that, in the late 1890s, the American Ornithologists' Union estimated five million birds were killed each year. Gene Stratton-Porter had long worn hats decorated with bird parts. But as she became aware of the massive slaughter, she resolved never to wear such bonnet trimmings again. She also decided to add her voice to the growing chorus of protesters.

Her protest began while on a shopping trip. After visiting several stores to find a suitable hat, one on which her "little feathered friends" were not mounted, she arrived at a fourth shop, feeling tired and cross. Not finding what she wanted, she nonetheless bought a hat and asked the shop owner for scissors. The hat contained "quite a little flight of birds," which Stratton-Porter immediately cut off and into pieces. The owner thought she was crazy; Stratton-Porter explained her action was "a question of conscience." Not long afterward, she submitted an article to the outdoor magazine *Recreation*, recounting her experience and suggesting that women's hats be trimmed in peacock feathers or ostrich plumes, which could be gathered without harming birds. Her article appeared in February 1900. At the age of thirty-six, she had finally launched her publishing career.

That same issue of *Recreation* carried a column by her titled "Camera Notes." Four years had passed since she first acquired a camera. By then, Stratton-Porter had studied nature long enough and mastered photography well enough to have ample material to submit for publication. Her birdlife articles and columns, along with photographs, began appearing regularly in *Recreation*. Beginning in July 1901 she also became a regular contributor to the outdoor magazine *Outing*.

Emboldened by her success, Stratton-Porter set a new goal. Remembering the pleasure she derived from writing fiction in high school, she decided to use her imagination again. At the time, readers craved tales featuring romance, kings and queens, and mythical kingdoms. To appeal to popular taste, Stratton-Porter wrote a short story titled "Laddie, the Princess, and the Pie." The setting was her own childhood farming community, not a castle. But she supplied the requisite romance and royalty by having a common boy fall in love with a well-born girl. Full of high hopes, she sent the story to *Metropolitan* magazine in New York. Weeks passed. Her hopes faded. She decided that the editor, Perriton Maxwell, "was a 'mean old thing' to throw away my story and keep the return postage."

Then one day, while downtown, one of Charles's employees told her he had read her story in *Metropolitan* the night before. Astonished, she bought the magazine, celebrated her story's publication in the September 1901 issue, and wrote to Maxwell saying she was glad he found it acceptable. He immediately wrote back, explaining that her return address had been lost and he had been unable to locate her. He enclosed payment and asked her to submit another story. She

A pensive Stratton-Porter ponders her next bit of writing. Responding to those who said her characters were too good, she noted: "I care very little for the . . . critics who proclaim that there is no such thing as a moral man, and that my pictures of life are sentimental and idealized. They are! And I glory in them!"

followed up with "How Laddie and the Princess Spelled Down at the Christmas Bee." When Maxwell asked for photographs to illustrate the story, Stratton-Porter rounded up local townsfolk, dressed them in 1870s-style costumes, and then worked through the night to develop the photos in time for the magazine's deadline. At four o'clock the next morning, she realized "I wanted a drink, food, and sleep, for I had not stopped a second for anything from the time of reading Mr. Maxwell's letter until his order was ready to mail."

That feverish pace might have caused some people to abandon publishing. But not Stratton-Porter. The next year, while still writing for *Metropolitan* and *Outing*, she sent a short story to Richard Watson Gilder, editor of *Century* magazine, one of the leading periodicals in the United States. He advised her to expand the tale into a novel. She spent a month reworking the story, then delivered it herself to Bobbs-Merrill, a thriving publishing company in Indianapolis. In the spring of 1903, Bobbs-Merrill published *A Song of the Cardinal*, a novel generously illustrated with her own photographs.

The story was inspired by a real-life incident. While walking along a road one afternoon, Stratton-Porter spotted the limp body of a redbird shot for target practice. Indignant about such a senseless killing, she took the bird home for burial. By the time she had finished scooping a deep grave, she had in her head the outline of story—that of a lovesick cardinal who narrowly escaped a hunter's bullet. Though the story was fiction, Stratton-Porter drew heavily from her vast knowledge of bird behavior. She also vividly described the Limberlost, where her protagonist the cardinal begins his life:

> The muck is alive with worms; and the whole swamp ablaze with flowers, whose colours and perfumes attract myriads of insects and butterflies. . . . Every hollow tree homes its colony of bats. Snakes

sun on the bushes. The water folk leave trails of shining ripples in their wake as they cross the lagoons. Turtles waddle clumsily from the logs. Frogs take graceful leaps from pool to pool. Everything native to that section of the country—underground, creeping, or a-wing—can be found in the Limberlost; but above all the birds.

Reviewers warmly praised the book, and readers liked it as well. But sales were sluggish and limited to a small audience. "The book started so slowly," Stratton-Porter recalled, "that soon I came to the realisation that if I could not reach people faster, so far as my work was concerned, the cardinals might all go as had the pigeons," a reference to flocks of passenger pigeons that once darkened the skies but had since been hunted to extinction. Stratton-Porter resolved not let her writing career grow extinct. She immediately wrote a second novel.

The Limberlost again served as her setting. But this time she placed people, not birds, at the heart of the story. The action centered on an Irish orphan named Freckles, who guards the Limberlost's valuable timber from thieves and falls in love with a pretty girl called the Swamp Angel. The story was inspired, in part, by the black vulture's nest that Stratton-Porter and Charles discovered. Freckles encounters just such a nest and enjoys the companionship of many birds, including a vulture named Little Chicken. Stratton-Porter wrote herself into the novel as a minor character. She is the "Bird Woman" who befriends Freckles and who, not surprisingly, photographs birds and wildlife in the swamp.

Published in 1904, *Freckles* received lukewarm reviews. "She has carried sentiment a trifle too far this time and made it ridiculous," wrote one critic. Another called *Freckles* a "very pleasing story" but disconnected from reality. In the Limberlost Swamp, that critic groused, "the world is younger and kinder than most people find it outside of enchanted places."

Readers, meanwhile, disagreed. Sales again were slow at first, but they steadily climbed as people discovered that *Freckles* was not strictly a nature book. Readers loved how Stratton-Porter combined light romance with a "whiff of the outdoors." Fan mail began to pour in from people of all ages and from all parts of the country. A reform-school warden wrote to say that fifteen hundred boys in his care could not put down their copies, worn ragged from use. A nurse writing from a hospital ward told of an invalid who enjoyed losing himself for an hour in Stratton-Porter's descriptions of forest and swamp. And a favorite letter came from the scholar and clergyman Oren Root, who paid her high tribute by writing: "I have a severe cold this morning, because I got my feet very wet last night walking the trail with

John James Audubon

'Freckles,' but I am willing to risk pneumonia any time for another book like that."

Stratton-Porter preferred to do most of her writing in the evenings. By day, she continued to travel up and down country roads, her camera equipment at the ready, her eyes and ears open to everything wild. She drove herself relentlessly. One day, after working outside in temperatures ranging between 104 and 108 degrees, she passed out in her buggy. Finding the horse and buggy tangled in a thicket of briers, an old farmer roused her and then scolded her for not having more sense. She accepted the scolding, but heeded not a word. Back she went, photographing birds in wetlands, woodlands, rivers, and pastures. She even snapped photos in barnyards, home to baby ducks. Her commitment to wildlife photography stemmed, in part, from her belief that photographs of birds were superior to the sketched illustrations in scientific bird guides. She also thought them superior to the drawings of John James Audubon, who achieved fame and fortune in the early 1800s as one of the first to paint lifelike images of North American birds in their natural surroundings.

Audubon's drawings, in Stratton-Porter's opinion, looked stiff, "as if they had been cut out with a scroll saw." She objected to his work for another reason, too. He and other illustrators collected birds for study purposes, and in the process often injured or killed them. At one point, she declared: "May heaven preserve me. No, may heaven preserve the birds" from those who deal in the "bloody work" of collecting. Having worked hard to master photography, she trusted her camera to deliver lifelike representations of birds. On good days, she hoped for even more, for something inexpressibly grand: "There comes a time in amateur photographic work when your plate is fresh and faultless, your light all you could wish, and your subject poses with a spirit as well as a body. In such cases you record, not details, but the light of the soul shining through the eyes."

Not long after *Freckles*'s publication, some of Stratton-Porter's photographs caught the attention of Edward Bok, editor of the *Ladies' Home Journal*, at that time America's leading women's magazine, the first in the nation to reach a million readers. A nature lover, Bok asked Stratton-Porter to meet him in Chicago. After viewing her portfolio of prints, he invited her to do a series of articles for the *Journal*.

Titled "What I Have Done with Birds," the series showcased Stratton-Porter's photographs, along with descriptions of bird life and how she secured the photos. The series ran from April to August 1906 and introduced Stratton-Porter's work to her largest audience to date. In 1907 the series was reprinted in book form by Bobbs-Merrill. The book did not sell briskly, but at least one academic reader, prominent paleontologist R. R. Rowley of Missouri, was impressed enough to take action. He named a trilobite for her: *Phillipsia Stratton-Porteri.*

Later in 1907, Stratton-Porter published her third novel, *At the Foot of the Rainbow.* Set along the Wabash River near a section called Rainbow Bottom, it is about two lifelong friends who enjoy fishing and trapping. One is preoccupied with acquiring material things. The other appreciates the beauty of the forest and the natural splendor of Rainbow Bottom, which he compares to an endless pot of gold. As in her earlier novels, Stratton-Porter included plentiful references to birds and, as one reviewer put it, "the changing pageant of the seasons." Like her earlier books, initial sales were disappointing.

But she remained too busy to worry about sales figures. For several years she had been poring over her Bible, making notes about passages that mentioned birds. She envisioned a book titled *Birds of the Bible,* to be illustrated with her own photographs. Her research led her on a "merry chase" through books, galleries, and museums to discover "the dawn of bird history, and the very first picture preserved ever made of birds." Her work also led her directly into the fields. As always, she spared no effort to get the photos she wanted. She burrowed into poison ivy vines to secure pictures of a brooding peacock. She hauled a dresser-top mirror outside and adjusted it to throw light so she could photograph a swallow's nest among the barn rafters. Stratton-Porter even endured lice raining down on her from various nests.

Cover of Stratton-Porter's 1907 book *What I Have Done with Birds*.

Cover of Stratton-Porter's 1909 book *Birds of the Bible*.

When it came time to publish *Birds of the Bible*, she urged Jennings and Graham, a religious publishing house in Cincinnati, to spare no expense. The result was impressive. The book was printed on heavy paper, contained eighty-one photographs, and had a simulated wood cover that Stratton-Porter designed. Upon the book's release in 1909, she assumed that ministers and churchgoers would embrace it and Sunday School teachers "would hail it as a Godsend in their work of interesting the young in the Bible." But sales again were slow, and Stratton-Porter conceded her miscalculation: "People did not think any of the things I thought they would."

That same year saw the publication of her fourth novel. Whatever her expectations for sales, she most certainly miscalculated again. *A Girl of the Limberlost* did more than sell well. It brought the Indiana nature lover worldwide fame.

6

When Gene Stratton-Porter sat down to write *A Girl of the Limberlost*, she envisioned a story that would do what *Freckles* did—uplift spirits and bring the outdoors to nature-starved readers, especially to the sick, troubled, and unfortunate. "I wrote [the book] to carry to workers inside city walls, to hospital cots, to those behind prison bars . . . my story of earth and sky," she said.

For her new novel, Stratton-Porter chose a familiar setting—the vast Limberlost wilderness. She also reintroduced characters, most notably the Bird Woman. But this story featured a determined young girl named Elnora Comstock whose widowed mother refuses to help her obtain an education. To earn money for her schooling, Elnora sells moths that she has collected from the Limberlost. When the money runs out, she must hunt for more moths and endure additional struggles. Along the way, however, romance flourishes, the mother's heart softens in the face of Elnora's natural goodness, and all ends well. As Stratton-Porter later wrote, "This comes fairly close to my idea of a good book. No possible harm can be done any one in reading it."

Critics saw little harm, either. The *New York Times Book Review* declared the book a "well written tale" in which the "heroine is a lovable young woman and gains the reader's sympathy at the start." *Booklist* was equally positive: "A bracing, wholesome story, with high

ideals and a pleasing outdoor atmosphere." Readers were even more
enthusiastic. As word of the book spread, sales skyrocketed—more than
ninety thousand copies sold in the first few years, and the numbers
climbed dramatically over the next decade. Total sales eventually topped
two million copies.

Inexpensive reprints of this book, along with *Freckles*, helped make
Stratton-Porter's name a household word and solidified her position as
one of America's most popular writers. Her international following also
soared. *A Girl of the Limberlost* became one of the first American novels
to be translated into Arabic. Translated editions also sold throughout
Europe and in Africa and Japan. Her overseas fans, like her American
counterparts, appreciated the book's romance, its nature lore, and the
lesson that virtue triumphs. And they could not resist saying thanks: "I
am only seventeen," a Yorkshire schoolgirl wrote Stratton-Porter. "No
doubt you have hundreds of letters similar to this, but I do ask you to
remember one girl in England who thinks you have the most beautiful
spirit possible."

As Stratton-Porter's career gained momentum in 1909, her family
life suffered a brief disruption. Jeannette surprised her parents by
announcing she was getting married—news neither parent welcomed.
Throughout Jeannette's childhood, the couple had carefully supervised
her upbringing. Stratton-Porter taught Jeannette how to tend a garden,
hunt for berries, and transplant wildflowers. Charles Porter instructed
her in how to fish, row a boat, shoot a rifle, and ride a horse. As
Jeannette grew, mother and daughter remained companions. Jeannette
accompanied Stratton-Porter into woods and fields, and, back at the
cabin, she typed her mother's articles and letters. "I was not allowed
to play much with the children of the town, so that when I was home
Mother spent considerable time with me," recalled Jeannette.

Eventually, however, Jeannette moved away from home—first to attend high school in Wabash (she boarded with relatives) and then college in Maryland. On returning to Indiana, she became infatuated with G. Blaine Monroe, a Pennsylvania oilman who had business dealings in Adams County. The Porters did not approve of Monroe and barred him from their home. Strong willed like her mother, Jeannette refused to call off the relationship, and in early February 1909 the young couple obtained a marriage license and prepared to elope. When Charles and Gene learned of the plans, they made hasty arrangements to have the couple wed at home. As to whether the marriage would last, Stratton-Porter continued to have reservations.

After the wedding, with the newlyweds off to their new life in the East, Stratton-Porter resumed her fieldwork and writing. She planned, and soon finished, another nature book, this one celebrating not just birds but also insects, flowers, trees, and landscapes. Titled *Music of the Wild*, the book carried a strong conservation message and warned, years before the Dust Bowl of the 1930s, how widespread destruction of trees and swamps could affect rainfall patterns. She explained how men greedy to cut

FROM THE COLLECTION OF THE INDIANA STATE MUSEUM AND HISTORIC SITES

Jeannette stands in front of some ferns at the Limberlost Cabin.

Publisher Frank Nelson Doubleday with his wife, Nellie, who was an author under the pen name Neltje Blanchan.

down forests can indirectly "cut down the clouds." This ambitious book was released in 1910 by Jennings and Graham, the firm that earlier published *Birds of the Bible*.

Somewhat predictably, reviewers panned the writing. "One finds chiefly bald description, dull enthusiasm, and ill-concealed sermons," declared *The Nation*. But that publication and others praised Stratton-Porter's camera work. *The Spectator*, a British magazine, declared that *Music of the Wild* is "illustrated with an extraordinary number of most excellent photographs, mostly of plants in natural surroundings."

Soon after the book's debut, Stratton-Porter made an important business decision. She reached a long-term publishing agreement with Doubleday, Page and Company—an arrangement that contributed to her growing popularity as a writer. Founded in 1900, the company was a leading New York City publishing house. When the company released *Freckles* in 1904, it already had a reputation for publishing books filled with nature lore. In 1910 Doubleday, Page boosted its "outdoors" image by becoming the first major publishing house to leave the crowded city and move to a more pastoral setting—thirty acres in the suburbs on Long Island. The cornerstone for the company's new headquarters was laid by Theodore Roosevelt, who as president had ardently championed wildlife conservation.

Publisher Frank N. Doubleday took a personal interest in Stratton-Porter. He did so with many of the company's best-selling authors, which included Edna Ferber, O. Henry, Sinclair Lewis, and Indianapolis native Booth Tarkington. Under the new arrangement, Doubleday, Page agreed to publish Stratton-Porter's novels *and* nonfiction books—one a year, on an alternating basis. Stratton-Porter preferred to write strictly nature books and believed that they, more than her fiction, would have lasting importance. Doubleday, however, understood the sales potential of her novels; he was willing to indulge her desire to write nonfiction, so long as a fiction book followed. He also was willing to commit advertising and publicity dollars to promote all her work. This arrangement proved mutually advantageous.

Doubleday, Page's advertising campaigns ramped up interest in Stratton-Porter's nonfiction work, allowing her to share her nature message with a broad audience. At the same time, her novels earned big profits for the company and confirmed Doubleday's judgment that his firm should represent her exclusively. As early as 1911, he received the confirmation he wanted. The company published *The Harvester*, Stratton-Porter's tale about a woodsman who sells plants for medicinal purposes. The novel shot to number five on the best-seller list, and the following year, 1912, it rose to number one. With the first edition quickly selling out, twenty-five thousand more copies were rushed into print.

While writing *The Harvester*, Stratton-Porter received a visit from Doubleday and his wife at her Limberlost Cabin. The Doubledays were among a growing number of people who appeared at her door. Although some were well-wishers hoping to meet the author, many others arrived carrying cocoons, bird nests, or unusual nature items they wanted her to identify. "Most of these interested callers I could ask to return at a later time," recalled Lorene Miller, who Stratton-Porter hired as her secretary in 1908. "But when I found someone at the cabin door with his hand cupped over the broken or injured body of a bird, I knew he was to be asked in."

With Miller in charge of keeping interruptions to a minimum, Stratton-Porter now spent her mornings writing fiction. After lunch, she napped. Regardless of the weather, she also took a walk. If too busy to take a long hike, she headed to a nearby bridge to do bending and stretching exercises. One day a woman who lived near the bridge asked Miller: "Jest what does that woman mean by them crazy moves on the bridge?" When Miller explained that Stratton-Porter needed to stretch after spending long hours at her desk, the woman replied: "Well, I jest 'lowed she'd worked her brain so hard she'd gone plum daffy."

October typically marked the start of the "book-making days," the time set aside for writing. Stratton-Porter wrote throughout the winter months, then devoted spring and summer to her fieldwork. Throughout the year, she committed a portion of her afternoon to reading fan mail, which grew more mountainous. She also read manuscripts from aspiring writers seeking her advice. "Her sympathetic heart would not allow her to return these manuscripts unread; after the most pressing of her own work was finished, she spent time and thought for the many who wrote her," Miller noted.

On winter evenings, seated before the fireplace, Stratton-Porter often read Charles and Miller a portion of what she had written that morning. Charles was a helpful sounding board. "Mrs. Porter always said her husband was one of her most expressive, if not her keenest of critics," said Miller. "If he did not like the manner in which the manuscript was written, in no uncertain tone Mr. Porter would point out, what to him, was the unconvincing phase of character drawing, or whatever might catch his critical ear." Heated arguments often ensued, with Stratton-Porter not always following her husband's advice. Still, Miller enjoyed "these literary fireworks" and observed that both "were always so sincere in their wish to help and be helped."

In 1912 Doubleday, Page abided by the new agreement and published Stratton-Porter's newest nature book, *Moths of the Limberlost*. Stratton-Porter's interest in moths had grown steadily during her years of fieldwork. She often collected cocoons in the woods, brought them home, and hung them among the flowers in her conservatory. Eventually, she began raising her own specimens to better study them. She even turned her bedroom into a hatchery and pinned cocoons close to her pillow at night. She did not want to miss being awakened by the scraping of feet when the moths—"these fragile night wanderers, these moon-flowers of June's darkness"—finally emerged. At the first sound, she grabbed her notebook and jotted down notes. Then over the

next several hours she photographed the moth's development from a thumbnail-sized creature to one attaining a wingspread of five to six inches.

As in her work with birds, Stratton-Porter believed it crucial that she photograph living moths. "Scientists from the beginning have had no hesitation in using dead and pinned moth specimens for book illustrations, despite the fact that the colours are faded, the wings in unnatural positions, and the body shrivelled," she said. "All the illustrations in my moth book are made from living moths and caterpillars in perfectly natural positions in which they placed themselves."

FROM THE COLLECTION OF THE INDIANA STATE MUSEUM AND HISTORIC SITES

Opposite: Moth featured on the title page of Stratton-Porter's 1912 book *Moths of the Limberlost*. "If only one person enjoys this book one-tenth as much as I have loved the work of making it," she said, "then I am fully repaid."
Above: A photograph of moths and their larvae by Stratton-Porter.

In 1912 color film had not yet been commercially produced; photographs were black and white or tinted brown. To help readers appreciate the delicate shading of moth wings and to aid collectors in identifying specimens, Stratton-Porter painted her prints using watercolors. She traveled to Indianapolis to buy a complete set of the finest paints and brushes available. She then hauled from her attic an easel her father had long ago given her. With painstaking care, she blended colors to match the nuanced hues of the moths' velvety wings. For greater precision, she even trimmed a brush down to three hairs. Jeannette, home on a visit with her new baby daughter, recalled how her mother would not stop until an illustration was finished: "I well remember that many times I stood beside Mother and fed her lunch to her, bite by bite, while she worked."

Of all her nature books, Stratton-Porter was most proud of *Moths of the Limberlost*. She believed it to be a practical guidebook—not as technical as other moth and butterfly books then on the market. She also savored the pleasure it gave her. "Never in all my life," she wrote, "have I had such exquisite joy in work as I had in painting the illustrations for this volume." She dedicated the book to Doubleday's wife, Neltje Blanchan, a well-known nature writer. The two had become friends and remained so until Blanchan's untimely death several years later. On receiving her copy of *Moths of the Limberlost*, Blanchan recognized the magnificence of the illustrations and sent her friend an appreciative note: "Nothing at the blessed Christmas season . . . touched me more than your dear gift. It is a veritable treasure, one that I shall be proud to pass on as an heirloom to future generations."

Stratton-Porter, meanwhile, had begun scouting for treasure of a different sort—namely, land to turn into a sanctuary for birds and wildlife and a place where she would have more privacy. In the summer

In her book on the moths of the Limberlost, Stratton-Porter encouraged people to welcome the creatures into their yards, noting: "I think people need not fear planting trees on their premises that will be favourites with caterpillars. . . . If you care for moths you need not fear to encourage them; the birds will keep them within proper limits."

of 1912, while vacationing as usual on Sylvan Lake, she found property to her liking on the lake's south shore. By October she had bought the land and was making plans for a new log cabin, amid a stand of hardwood trees. She was forty-nine years old. By her reckoning, it was time for a new adventure.

7

When Gene Stratton-Porter made the decision to move north to Sylvan Lake, her beloved Limberlost Swamp had all but vanished. By the early 1900s, loggers had cut down most of the trees, selling the tall timber to shipbuilders, hardwood to furniture factories, and softwood to barrel makers. As the timber was removed, brush was burned, wiping out plant and wildlife. Oil and gas drillers swarmed in and hastened the destruction. By 1909 roughly 650 wells were pumping in the region, producing more than a million barrels of oil annually. Farmers launched their own assault by digging ditches, laying clay tiles, and straightening creeks. On land once swampy, they planted fields of onions, celery, and sugar beets.

Stratton-Porter was not opposed to economic growth, and she understood that oil wells were a source of Charles Porter's wealth. However, the wholesale destruction of wildlife and wild places, with no thought given to conservation, appalled her. As she told her readers: "Now it [Limberlost] has so completely fallen prey to commercialism through the devastation of lumbermen, oilmen, and farmers, that I have been forced to move my working territory and build a new cabin about seventy miles north."

The move did not happen overnight. In the spring of 1913, Stratton-Porter hired Frank Wallace, a tree surgeon and later state

Philip Wesley Smith and Jacob Colter expanded their lumber company, Colter and Company, located in Arcola, by opening two mills in Adams County and one in Decatur under the name Adams County Lumber Company. Sales were mostly to railroad companies.

entomologist, to inspect her new property—initially five acres of forest and blue-eyed grass. She knew she needed healthy trees to attract birdlife and to establish the wildlife preserve she desired. Wallace's assignment, with the aid of a crew of men, was to clear away diseased and dead timber, fill tree cavities, and replace poison vines and nonflowering plants with those bearing fruits and berries. Hollow trees were left standing; Stratton-Porter wanted to encourage raccoons, owls, squirrels, and rabbits to stay and make homes.

A cedar-log cabin, a larger version of the one at Geneva, was planned near the shoreline. The cabin was intended to be both a home and a workshop, complete with a photographic darkroom and printing room. Stratton-Porter had earlier bought a summer cottage across the lake, allowing her to stay and supervise construction at the new site. "I lived on the job," she noted, "from the drawing of the line for the back steps between the twin oaks to the last stroke of polish that finished the floors." She even helped design and build the fireplaces in the living room and the library. Her design called for the use of an attractive local stone known as pudding stone, which she trekked about the countryside to find.

Behind the house, Stratton-Porter marked out areas for a vegetable garden, a cultivated flower garden, and an orchard. On the rest of the property, which with additional purchases grew to 120 acres, she determined that nothing but "wild" things should be planted. By then, northern Indiana farmers were pushing to drain wetlands to create tillable fields, just as Geneva-area farmers had done. Having seen the destruction of her Limberlost and aware of the consequences of ditch digging, Stratton-Porter feared that the region's rare and delicate wildflowers would be threatened with extinction. During the next

Stratton-Porter with her car loaded down with plants she had collected.

six years, she traveled throughout northern Indiana rescuing these endangered plants, braving everything from quicksand to rattlesnakes and poison ivy. Sometimes she hired a crew of men and their wagons to haul the specimens back to her estate. More often, she transformed her seven-passenger automobile, which replaced her horse and buggy, into a type of truck. She loaded ferns and flowers into a big storage chest located in the back seats. She placed similar wildings in boxes attached to the running boards. As if that were not enough, Stratton-Porter noted: "Frequently I threw coffee sacking over the engine hood and loaded it with swamp mosses and bulbous plants, with pitcher plant and rosemary, as high as I could stack it and allow space for the driver to see over."

Back on her property, named Wildflower Woods, she set most of the plants herself. "I am rather new at the flower business. My forte is birds and moths," Stratton-Porter wrote at one point to Wallace. Still, she had learned much about growing things from her mother, and most of the transplanted specimens survived. In the first few years, she brought more than three thousand trees, shrubs, vines, and wildflowers to her estate. As more people, including her readers, learned of her efforts to save wildflowers, admirers began sending her packets of seeds and rare plants from around the world. Over time, the cast of colorful and fragrant wildflowers came to include buttercups, fringed gentians, purple asters, red wood lilies, white trillium, and starry campions. She could pinpoint each one because, as Wallace noted, "she had been on her knees on almost every square foot of ground in the woods surrounding her cabin."

As work progressed at her cabin and the grounds, readers enjoyed Stratton-Porter's newest novel, *Laddie: A True Blue Story*, which was

Top: Workers involved in the construction of Stratton-Porter's new home in Rome City, Indiana, pose on its front porch. Stratton-Porter closely supervised work on her home. She even hosted Thanksgiving dinner for the workers in November 1913. A newspaper noted that "the event proved most pleasing to all present. The turkey was sent from New York and the apples were prize winners at the Indiana state fair." By mid-February 1914, after some "unlooked for delays," the home was ready for occupancy. **Above:** The home's arbor and cultivated gardens.

published in the summer of 1913 and became another best seller. It was inspired by memories of her brother, Laddie, about whom she had written years earlier in her short story. Although the book was fiction, Stratton-Porter intended it to closely represent her childhood on the farm: "I could write no truer biography. To the contour of hill and field, to the last stripe on the wallpaper and knot on the door, that is the home in which I was born." For critics, the novel's sentimentality and lecturing tone again proved to be too much. "There is a great deal of preaching, virtue is rewarded right and left," complained the *New York Times* reviewer. A British reviewer bristled that Laddie and his family were "all human perfection," which is why "we should find them intolerably wearisome."

By then, Stratton-Porter also was bristling, thoroughly frustrated with those who found her fiction too sweet. To her detractors, she replied: "To-day a criticism of *Laddie* by a minister of the Gospel was sent me in which he wrote of it as 'molasses fiction.' What a wonderful compliment! All the world loves sweets. . . . Molasses is more necessary to the happiness of human and beast than vinegar, and over-indulgence not nearly so harmful to the system. I am a molasses person myself. . . . So are most of my friends—all of them who are happy, as a matter of fact. So I shall keep straight on writing of the love and joy of life I have found in the world. . . . God gave me a taste for sweets and the

A common view of Stratton-Porter—surrounded by plants outdoors.

sales of the books I write prove that a few other people are similar to me in this."

Throughout her career, Stratton-Porter refused to allow criticism to distract her for long. Fieldwork continued to occupy her time, as did overseeing the finishing touches on the cabin. In February 1914 she finally moved in. Charles, then in his sixties, remained in Geneva to attend to his business affairs, though he took the train to Rome City on weekends. With cabin crowding not an issue, secretary Lorene Miller became a permanent houseguest.

The cabin's upstairs had seven bedrooms and one-and-a-half baths, along with sleeping porches on three sides of the house. From those porches, Stratton-Porter could closely observe and hear the birds that took sanctuary in her woods. Downstairs, she took in other pleasing sites—rooms paneled in wild cherry, elaborate fireplaces, a modern kitchen, cabinets for her photographic equipment and negatives, and breathtaking views of lake and forest from the large living-room window.

Within weeks, she wrote to Wallace: "On snowy days Lorene and I go from window to window to see the picture of the snow gracefully whirling through the big trees in Wildflower Woods and nights of white moonlight are so lovely the sight actually hurts." She had not yet taken any nature photographs, but she told Wallace: "I've seen signs and wonders and miracles in Wildflower Woods this winter just waiting to be recorded with my camera in the spring."

The arrival of spring brought good news of another sort—the birth of Stratton-Porter's granddaughter. Eager to spend time with Jeannette and her growing family, Stratton-Porter and Charles traveled in the fall to Philadelphia, where Jeannette's husband, Blaine Monroe, had just started his university studies to become a dentist. One afternoon, a newsboy tried to sell Stratton-Porter a newspaper. She and her family were hurrying home from a shopping trip and paid no attention to him. But as Jeannette later recalled, the newsboy was a good salesman. He ran alongside Stratton-Porter and told her what a kind face she had. "This was too much," Jeannette remembered. "Mother bought all his papers and sent him off with enough money to buy a supper for his entire family." The little newsboy became the inspiration for her next novel, *Michael O'Halloran*, whose central character was an orphaned lad named Mickey trying to support himself while living on the streets.

Unlike her earlier novels, this one—published in August 1915—was set in a large midwestern city. Try though she did, her descriptions of slum life were not entirely convincing. "The tenement room shared by Mickey and Lily Peaches [an orphaned girl Mickey befriends] is nestlike, almost pleasant," the author Bertrand Richards commented years later. Still, Stratton-Porter's loyal readers loved the story. And her message of clean living continued to strike a chord. "Less than five minutes ago I laid it [the book] down. Thank you. I've ended the story. But Mickey will remain with me through the days," wrote a man about to be released from prison. Stratton-Porter, meanwhile, remained committed to giving readers a feel for the outdoors. In *Michael O'Halloran*, she described a swamp near the city—a place remarkably like the marshy Indiana landscape she knew so well:

> Here the moss lay in a flat carpet, tinted deeper green. Water willow rolled its ragged reddish-tan hoops, with swelling bloom and leaf buds. Overflowing pitcher plants grew in irregular beds, on slender stems, lifting high their flat buds. But scattered in groups here and there . . . stood the rare, early fringed orchis, some almost white, others pale lavender and again the deeper colour of the moccasins.

At the close of 1915, Stratton-Porter hurried to the bedside of her seriously ill brother, Lemon, who lived in southern Indiana. He died during the Christmas holidays from heart disease. Lemon, who had married three times, left his twelve-year-old daughter, Leah Mary, to his sister to raise. "I shall have one more little girl to love and help all I can," Stratton-Porter wrote to a friend. Leah Mary moved to Wildflower Woods, where she remained for several years. Her youthful presence in the cabin was matched by Stratton-Porter's two granddaughters, who Jeannette brought to Indiana for extended visits. Stratton-Porter loved photographing the girls. She also loved teaching them about nature.

In October 1916 Doubleday, Page published *Morning Face*, a collection of light, sing-song verse and amusing stories Stratton-Porter wrote for children and illustrated with her nature photos. Included were photographs of her first grandchild, Jeannette Helen, who as an infant had been lovingly nicknamed "Morning Face." In sharing the book with a friend, Stratton-Porter said she had refrained from writing down to youngsters: "The Natural History is right and true, I hope, lightened by gleams of humour which I find distressingly rare in books for children." A reviewer for *The Literary Digest* noted the "gleams" and agreed with Stratton-Porter's overall point: "There is a quaint humor, every now and then, peeping out between the irregular lines of the verse, and that is something in these days when humor is so lacking in our juvenile literature."

Stratton-Porter saw nothing humorous, however, about what was happening in Noble County and neighboring Lagrange County around that time. More and more ditches were being cut, lowering lake levels and directly threatening the region's wildlife. When she learned a law was being proposed to drain state-owned swampland in those two counties—a law the Indiana General Assembly passed in 1917—her anger boiled over: "I was horrified. Drying up the springs, drying up the streams, and lowering the lake meant to exterminate the growth by running water, meant to kill the great trees that had flourished since the beginning of time around the borders of the lakes, meant to kill the vines and shrubs and bushes, the ferns and the iris and the water hyacinths, the arrowhead lilies and the rosemary and the orchids, and it meant, too, that men were madly and recklessly doing an insane thing without really understanding what they were doing."

With little time to waste, Stratton-Porter immediately redoubled her efforts to save native plants by bringing them to Wildflower Woods. She also led an effort to repeal the law and to educate citizens on the need for fast action. "Life became one round of fight," she wrote. "Fight from morning until night . . . fight for the conservation of physical and spiritual comfort and of hunt, seek, and search to rescue every one of these delicate little blossoms possible before destruction overtook them." The law was repealed in 1920. The swampland, however, was later drained.

Wildflower Woods, meanwhile, grew lusher. Much of the pride Stratton-Porter felt for her estate and her spacious cabin came from the fact that it was entirely hers—paid for with the income from her books. She had not relied on Charles for money; she was financially independent. "There is a sort of heady exhilaration," she explained, "about being able to look the world in the face and feel that you are equal to it; that you can take care of yourself, and others if necessary, by your own individual efforts."

As her fame grew, Stratton-Porter had to intensify efforts to protect her privacy, and she eventually posted "No Admittance" signs around her estate. In spite of these precautions, the curious came to visit. "There would often be as many as twenty-five cars on the grounds at one time and it was sometimes very embarrassing to have fifty or more people walk past and look us over while we were eating our dinner out in the yard," Wallace recalled. Once, visitors from Canada approached as Stratton-Porter was bent over in her orchid bed. They asked if she worked for Mrs. Porter. Wishing not to draw attention to herself, she said yes, at which point they asked if the famous author was kind, if she paid her workers well, and if her house was beautifully furnished. To end the questioning, Stratton-Porter finally suggested they should go see the other flower beds, after which she hurried into the cabin. Recounted Wallace: "She often laughed about her predicament and wondered what she would have done if one of them had recognized her."

While gawkers were not always welcome on her estate, wild birds were. She worked especially hard to preserve great horned owls, a pair of which lived in the hollow of a large beech tree near her cabin. The owls, which stood nearly two feet in height and had a four- to five-foot wingspan, were despised by one of Stratton-Porter's neighbors because they killed his chickens. Whenever one of his flock was destroyed, the neighbor would place arsenic near the beech tree. "Nearly every evening, before time for the owls' flight, I would slip through the woods, sneak [the farmer's] bait, and carry it away," she wrote to friends.

In the same letter, she told of her close encounter in the woods with "monkey-faced" barn owls, known for their penetrating cry. "I went out to call on them the other night, and I think nothing but a white dress I was wearing saved me from having them launch themselves upon my head, as they swooped down very close to me, screaming with anger." She took all such encounters in stride: "You know, I have a theory that one must not upset the balance of Nature. One must leave her in her natural state to work out her own salvation."

In 1917 Stratton-Porter completed a revised and enlarged version of *What I Have Done with Birds*, published a decade earlier. This new version, released by Doubleday, Page, was titled *Friends in Feathers*. Like the rest of the nation, however, her attention was sharply diverted in the spring. For nearly three years, European nations had been at war, and on April 2, 1917, President Woodrow Wilson declared the United States should join the conflict to make the world "safe for democracy." Four days later, Congress issued a formal war declaration.

Like other patriotic Americans, Stratton-Porter dutifully observed new food regulations the government put in place; she and her

President Woodrow Wilson addresses Congress in 1917. On April 2 that year Wilson declared the United States should enter World War I on the Allied side against Germany.

household refrained from eating "meat" or "wheat" on certain days to allow for more food to be shipped overseas. She also required every household member, including her cook, to knit for the soldiers. With her field workers off to military service, she no longer had men to help maintain the cabin and grounds, no man except Charles, who still came only on weekends. She was especially sad when her chauffeur Bill Thompson enlisted. To a friend, she described how valuable Thompson had been to her: "We put in three summers of field work, collecting, lifting, transplanting rare plants from where we motored to find them all over our State. He carried cameras and helped in picture work and drove my car. He was a straight, honest, brave lad. . . . I mothered him as I do all boys; but not all are of such fine timbre."

As the fall of 1917 gave way to a bitter winter, and as news from overseas remained grim, Stratton-Porter felt out of sorts: "My beautiful optimism is getting many a severe jolt these days," she observed. She worked to make Christmas festive by hanging holly wreaths in the windows, draping the mantels with Spanish moss and pine, and trimming three Christmas trees—in the library, in the dining room, and on the porch outside her conservatory. The outdoor tree was for birds and squirrels. She hung little wire containers on the branches and filled them with scraped beef, seeds, nuts, and bones with bits of gristle. She added yards of strung popcorn and pieces of apple and orange, which she replenished daily. "There was no lovelier sight than the brilliantly coloured birds as they chirped to each other while they ate greedily," recalled Jeannette.

After the holidays, Stratton-Porter continued to scatter food outside her conservatory window. "Uncounted chickadees, titmice, nut hatches, sapsuckers, flickers, song sparrows, jays, and cardinals, and a pair of squirrels are holding high carnival," she wrote to a friend. It was definitely a *winter* carnival: "The big forest trees are frost-laden, the lake a sheet of ice, the ground almost a foot deep in snow, and a big blizzard blowing straight from the east. This is 'Back to Nature' with a vengeance." Stratton-Porter wanted no more vengeance: "I am perfectly crazy for spring to come over the hill."

8

In the early months of 1918, Gene Stratton-Porter put the finishing touches on a new novel. If it ever occurred to her to write about the war and its heartaches, she chose not to. Instead, *A Daughter of the Land* was about a country girl who overcomes obstacles to get what she always yearned for, a farm of her own. The book sold well, though not like her earlier work had done.

Critics, for the most part, were satisfied. A reviewer for *Publishers Weekly* called the novel "notable because it is simple and elemental, because it has sincerity and breadth." William Lyon Phelps, a lecturer at Yale and one of the nation's most respected critics, found even more to praise: "I defy any unprejudiced person to read *A Daughter of the Land* to the end, without enthusiasm for the story . . . the heroine is a girl that holds one's attention, not merely by what happens to her, but by what she is. . . . Here was a girl who really loved the country; loved living on a farm; loved all kinds of agricultural work; loved to make and see things grow. And, as presented in the novel, this love is understandable and intelligible. There are not many such girls. But it would be well if there were more."

As was her custom when the weather turned balmy, Stratton-Porter resumed her forays into swamps and marshes, always bringing more flowers to her wooded estate. She also delighted in seeing the previous

year's plantings thrive. "The orchid bed we made turned out to be a glowing success," she wrote to a friend. "And of the big six-foot tall ferns I moved in, only two failed me and the others are from four to six inches higher than the ones in the swamp from which I took them." The fieldwork was taking its toll on her, however. She turned fifty-five that summer, and her once boundless energy gave way to fatigue. Concerned about her overall health, she traveled in the fall to upstate New York. She checked into the Clifton Springs Sanitarium and Clinic, a fashionable spa where people went to rest and bathe in sulphur springs, believed to have healing powers.

Feeling restored, she left after a month. But instead of pampering herself, Stratton-Porter launched into more backbreaking projects. In ten days, she and Frank Wallace planted 1,204 flowers, vines, shrubs, and trees on her property. Next, she built a pair of nine-foot-tall gateposts at the road entrance to her estate, using leftover pudding stone. She then headed down to the lake, where she built a small stone wall around a natural spring near the shoreline, before returning indoors to tackle the semiannual housecleaning. "Frequently I was so tired I could scarcely get to the cabin at night," she said regarding the gatepost project. But like most Americans, she had reason to rejoice as 1918 drew to a close. On November 11, a defeated Germany signed an armistice ending World War I. Four days later, Stratton-Porter wrote to a friend: "We are overjoyed with the prospect of the end of the war coming nearer, so we can begin to plan to live once more, in some respects, as we did in the good old days."

Opposite: Talking about her writing, Stratton-Porter observed: "For every bad man and woman I have ever known, I have met . . . an overwhelming number of thoroughly clean and decent people who still believe in God and cherish high ideals, and it is upon the lives of these people that I base what I write. To contend that this does not produce a picture true to life is idiocy."

But the coming days were not all good. People in nearly every part of the world were suffering and dying from influenza, an infectious disease also known as the "Spanish Flu." The flu pandemic lasted from March 1918 to June 1920, leaving millions dead. Stratton-Porter herself was stricken: "I ended by breaking down with the Flu with no nurse and a doctor forty miles away." But she was fortunate enough to recover, and by the spring of 1919 she was pushing to finish a new nature book.

The idea for the book had been suggested three years earlier by her friend Neltje Blanchan, who had encouraged Stratton-Porter to compile stories of her many unusual experiences in the field—her observation of the robin that had blistered its throat eating poison berries, the oriole that had hanged itself on the string with which it was building its nest, the young blackbird that squalled so loudly a hen robin eventually fed it. Stratton-Porter took her friend's advice and wrote *Homing with the Birds*. In chapters ranging from courtship to nest building, she described the habits and characteristics of birds in simple language, careful not to "over-humanize" them. She also detailed how she secured rare photographs and concluded one chapter with a plea to protect not only birds but all wildlife: "If men do not take active conservation measures soon, I shall be forced to enter politics to plead for the conservation of the forests, wildflowers, the birds, and over and above everything else, the precious water on which our comfort, fertility, and life itself depend."

Homing with the Birds was published in the fall of 1919. A reviewer for the *New York Times* insisted "no one who has any interest in the feathered denizens of the air can afford to miss her book." *The Spectator* agreed, calling it "a capital book." But it was praise from the distinguished writer and editor Christopher Morley that pleased Stratton-Porter the most. In a letter sent to her publisher, Morley wrote: "Mrs. Porter's beautiful stories of her bird friends . . . are a kind of education in the art of wondering at the fulness of life. They refresh the sense of amazement." Morley said he considered her work with birds to be on par with the insect studies of the famous French entomologist Jean-Henri Fabre. "Please pardon this outburst!" Morley concluded his letter. "It is a spontaneous utterance of admiration for Mrs. Porter's unique gift of fellowship with the birds, which seems to have been born in her warm and courageous heart."

Stratton-Porter, meanwhile, was thinking about refreshing *her* senses. She had grown tired of severe winters and was attracted to the notion of year-round sunshine. Her thoughts drifted to Southern California, where her oldest sister, Catherine, and other relatives lived. By the summer of 1919, she began making serious plans about moving west, at least for a season or two. In October, she was ready. She traveled to Los Angeles and rented a small house. After six weeks, she bought a bungalow in Hollywood, not far from where Catherine resided. Stratton-Porter did not abandon Wildflower Woods, but she was in no hurry to head back. "I sorter like this glorious sunshine, the pergola of Cherokee roses, the orange trees and blood red poinsettias, and the mocking birds tame as robins at home," she wrote to a friend.

Six months later, she returned to Indiana, burdened by the news that Jeannette's troubled marriage was unraveling. Then living in Fort Wayne, Jeannette filed for divorce that summer. In October 1920 the divorce was official, and Jeannette was granted full custody of her daughters. By late fall all four of them—Stratton-Porter, Jeannette, and the young girls—were in Los Angeles. Stratton-Porter bought a house ten miles from the ocean. It had enough room for the girls and for Charles Porter, though he remained in Geneva, still involved in his bank.

Taking her usual pride in her property, Stratton-Porter wasted no time sprucing up the residence. "It required some fresh papering, floor waxing, woodwork cleaning, and glass washing. Much new furniture had to be selected, curtains made and hung—oh, such a lot of work!" she wrote to friends at Christmas. "But we are nearly enough settled. . . . I think this purchase means that this will be home in the winter hereafter."

In ways she had never done in Indiana, Stratton-Porter began socializing. She made a point of getting to know the "locals" in their homes and at parties, declaring the experience to be broadening and interesting. Afternoons and evenings found her attending luncheons, receptions, dinners, and "entertainments." Her new circle of acquaintances included a wide range of artists, from actors and musicians to sculptors and poets. For all the worldliness and wealth of these "fine folk," as she called them, she refused to let them intimidate her: "I stand up and speak my little piece with the best of them without a bat of the eye or a quiver of an eyelash." Stratton-Porter did, however, feel obligated to spice up her wardrobe. "I have lain aside boots and breeches and put on crepe and beaded chiffon and a French bonnet with roses and a veil," she said.

Doubleday, Page published no Stratton-Porter books in 1920. But by January 1921, she was back in print. *Good Housekeeping*, a women's magazine with a national circulation, published a poem she penned

Opposite: Stratton-Porter and her brother, Jerome Stratton, show off some of the results from a five-day fishing trip they took at Santa Catalina Island off the southern coast of California in 1924. The photograph was featured in *American Magazine.*

about birdlife. Another of her poems appeared in *Good Housekeeping* in May. In August her new novel, *Her Father's Daughter*, was released. It was about a seventeen-year-old who learned from her father to appreciate the beauty of her surroundings, though not the usual woods and swamps of Indiana. Instead, Stratton-Porter lavishly depicted Southern California's mountains, canyons, desert, and gardens, getting advice on the region's plant life from her niece's husband, James Sweetser Lawshe: "To whom I owe all that I know about the flowers of California."

Charles Dorwin Porter sits on a bench with a canine companion. "No one in the whole world knows all a man's bignesses and all his littlenesses as his wife does," noted Stratton-Porter.

Not all was beautiful within *Her Father's Daughter*, however. Though a newcomer to the West Coast, Stratton-Porter had quickly soaked up the region's bias against Chinese and Japanese citizens. She played to popular prejudice by portraying the novel's Asian characters as being inferior to whites. Phelps, the Yale lecturer who had admired Stratton-Porter's *A Daughter of the Land*, took her to task for her latest book: "In addition to the literary shortcomings of this novel, it is sadly marred by anti-Japanese propaganda. Somebody in California has been stuffing our novelist, who is more gullible in international politics than in the study of nature."

Despite a busy schedule in 1921, Stratton-Porter took time to vacation in Indiana, with her youngest granddaughter joining her for the summer. Later that year, back in California, she received a visit from Harry Burton, the editor of *McCall's*. He had traveled to Los Angeles expressly to persuade her to write a series of monthly editorials for the magazine's female audience, which was growing under his direction.

Stratton-Porter hesitated at first. "She felt that *McCall's* might be just a little below the level in literary values of the other magazines to which she had been contributing," Jeannette recalled. But Burton insisted that *McCall's* readers needed to hear the commonsense wisdom she could deliver. Persuaded, Stratton-Porter signed a contract to supply editorials for one year, the first appearing in *McCall's* January 1922 issue.

As a columnist, her goal was straightforward. Stratton-Porter wanted to make American women feel good about being mothers and housewives at a time when homemaking was being devalued. She doled out advice on everything from raising children to caring for relatives, from having fun without money to growing old gracefully. She preached her usual message, too, urging readers to venture outdoors and appreciate nature. "Gene Stratton-Porter's Page," as her column was known, caught on quickly, and subscriptions to the magazine grew. When Burton returned to California to urge her to sign another year's contract, she did, with other contracts following.

Burton's personality appealed to Stratton-Porter. She especially approved of his editorial judgment and business smarts—his ability to make the once-struggling *McCall's* profitable. "I take extreme pride in the way that magazine has grown during the past three years," she wrote to her book publisher, "and I hope that we shall be able to go on until we put McCall's at the top of American publications." Judging from

the feedback of grateful readers, Stratton-Porter contributed mightily to the magazine's success. "From women in lonely ranch houses, from wardens of prisons, from pastors and educators, from young girls and boys, from brides and mothers, have come thousands and thousands of letters telling what Gene Stratton-Porter meant to them," *McCall's* editors later wrote. "[Her] messages, given sincerely, courageously, and truthfully, from a great wealth of personal experience, found their way to the heart of America."

Opposite: Stratton-Porter in the outdoors of California about 1924.

9

Before World War I, most American movies were produced in New York City and New Jersey, and to a lesser extent in places such as Chicago, Illinois. Increasingly, movie producers realized that Southern California's sunny climate offered them the opportunity to film year-round, prompting many to head west. Soon, the Hollywood district of Los Angeles became a popular place to open film studios. After the war, Hollywood became the motion picture capital of the world.

Gene Stratton-Porter had already had one experience with the film industry. In 1917 Paramount produced *Freckles* as a movie. She had given her permission, with the understanding that she could offer ideas on how to adapt her novel to the screen. But her suggestions were ignored and the movie did not follow the novel. Hating the result, Stratton-Porter vowed that no more pictures would be made from her books, at least until she had more control over the screenplays.

Still, the movie companies kept contacting Stratton-Porter. Upon her arrival in California in 1919, they besieged her with requests to sell the film rights to her books. "At first she was not particularly interested, and refused them all point-blank without even an interview," said her daughter, Jeannette. But in 1921 Stratton-Porter struck a deal with a filmmaker named Thomas Ince, whose slogan was "Clean Pictures for Clean People." She granted Ince's company the movie rights to her

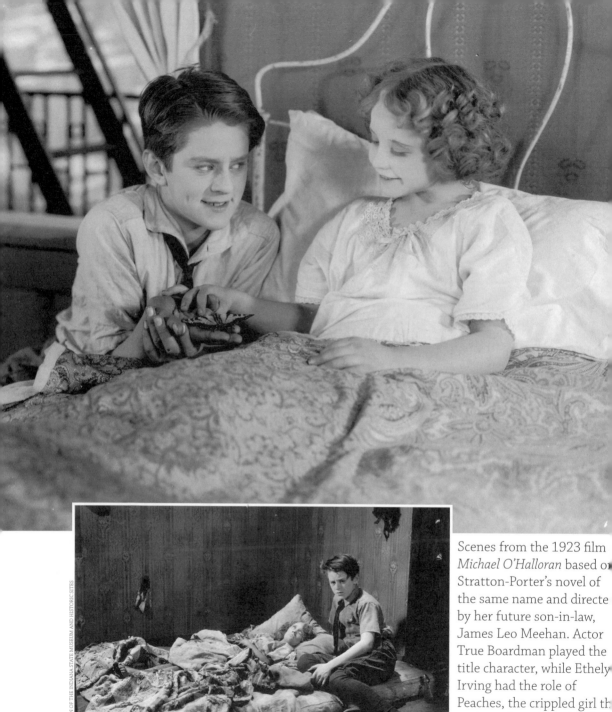

Scenes from the 1923 film *Michael O'Halloran* based on Stratton-Porter's novel of the same name and directe by her future son-in-law, James Leo Meehan. Actor True Boardman played the title character, while Ethely Irving had the role of Peaches, the crippled girl th orphaned Mickey O'Hallora takes in as a member of his family.

novel *Michael O'Halloran*, with the agreement that Jeannette would write the screenplay and Stratton-Porter would oversee the filming. The arrangement also allowed Stratton-Porter to assist the young director, James Leo Meehan, to whom she took an instant liking.

As she did with any new project, Stratton-Porter threw herself into filmmaking. She arrived on the movie set early each morning and stayed until the evening hours. She made a point of getting to know *everyone*, not just the actors, and enjoyed herself thoroughly. People in the movie industry had forewarned her there was not a large market for wholesome family entertainment. They also warned it would be difficult to find organizations to distribute her brand of films and to get theaters to exhibit them. "She was assured . . . [her films] would not be popular because there was not sufficient action, there were no hair-raising thrills, there were no violent sex problems, and there was too much Nature and too much 'sugary romance,'" recalled Jeannette.

Despite the warnings, Stratton-Porter did not waver. She made sure *Michael O'Halloran* faithfully dramatized the morally uplifting message in her novel, and she celebrated as the film successfully premiered in Los Angeles in 1923. Feeling vindicated, she launched into producing her next "clean" film, *A Girl of the Limberlost*.

By then, she had decided to go solo. In January 1924 she formed her own movie company, Gene Stratton-Porter Productions, with Meehan as director. Six months earlier, Stratton-Porter had welcomed Meehan into the family; he and Jeannette had married in June. Stratton-Porter's vision for her new company was to make films "of men and women who inspire charity, honor, devotion to God and to family"—a vision she had earlier outlined in a *McCall's* editorial. Realizing the cultural forces she was up against, Stratton-Porter immediately sought to enlist women in her cause.

Title plates and individual scenes from the films *A Girl of the Limberlost* (1934), starring Louise Dresser, and *Romance of the Limberlost* (1938), featuring Marjorie Main. Both Main and Dresser were Hoosier actresses.

In a letter to the president of a national clubwomen's organization, Stratton-Porter was blunt: "The only way in all this world through which we can have better pictures is for more people to patronize better pictures. . . . When you stop to consider that picture making is the third largest industry in the United States to-day and that a bad picture reaches more people than any other one medium, certainly it is worth while for the women who are trying to better conditions to take hold of the picture question."

In that same letter, she detailed her efforts to promote "decency" on the screen and issued a rallying cry. Referring to *A Girl of the Limberlost*, Stratton-Porter observed: "Every dollar of money that went into this picture I earned myself, most of it in the fields and woods and in the swamps, much of the time on my knees. . . . Now if the club women, the school women, and the church women, will stand by me, we can prove to the public what kind of a picture people really want."

That appeal, and others Stratton-Porter made when asked to speak at women's conventions, paid off for *A Girl of the Limberlost.* By late summer of 1924, the film drew huge crowds to Graumann's, a big theater in downtown Los Angeles. "The managers of the theatre tell me that it has done the best business of any picture since they had control of the theatre," Stratton-Porter informed a friend. "And . . . on Labour Day they had the biggest house and made the most money . . . in the history of the theater."

As enthusiastic as she was about making movies, Stratton-Porter felt another urge bubbling up inside her. She had always loved poetry and had wished to write more of it. Now, in her new surroundings, she decided to "bust loose" and allow her brain to go "whirling off at this new tangent." Her first effort was a long narrative poem, *The Fire Bird*, written in just three days. It was inspired by photographs she had

seen of American Indians and by a folk legend about a cardinal. Books
of poetry were not moneymakers; that was well understood within the
publishing industry. Even so, Stratton-Porter's standing was so high
at Doubleday, Page that the company published *The Fire Bird* in
April 1922.

To ensure the book's success, Stratton-Porter asked her friends to
help with promotion. To an acquaintance in Winchester, Indiana, she
wrote: "I want you to constitute yourself an amateur book agent and
see what you can do for the sale of this volume among your friends."
Sales were not strong, and her friends were likely as dismayed as she was
with the reviews. *Booklist* insisted that Stratton-Porter "is not a poet"
and said *The Fire Bird* "does not possess a single line . . . containing that
divine substance which we call poetry."

Even before *The Fire Bird*'s release, Stratton-Porter was writing,
and rewriting, another long poem titled *Euphorbia*. It told the story of
a woman in a loveless marriage who eventually found reason to hope.
The poem's title came from a desert plant that the woman cares for, sees
destroyed, and then watches grow again. Beginning in January 1923,
this new poem appeared in three installments in *Good Housekeeping*
magazine amid much fanfare and with lavish display. The first
installment bore the caption: "Gene Stratton-Porter, whose name on
the title pages of nearly ten million books entitles her to be called The
Most Popular Woman Writer in the World."

As she had done in *The Fire Bird*, Stratton-Porter wrote *Euphorbia*
in blank verse. Instead of following traditional poetic forms, she
intended for the rhythms of the verse to come from feelings and ideas
within the poem—a style of poetry considered modern. Her sister
Catherine weighed in on *Euphorbia* well before other critics: "It's a
heart-breaking story. It flows the smoothest of anything I ever read in
print, but for God's sake don't publish that and call it poetry!"

But Stratton-Porter had no interest in shaking the "poetry virus." A third poem soon followed, inspired by a legend that the Roman emperor Tiberius Caesar had ordered the likeness of Christ's face to be carved on an emerald. Years earlier, while researching her book *Birds of the Bible*, Stratton-Porter had come across the legend. She was reminded of it when she received a letter and a photograph— purportedly of the ancient emerald—from one of her readers in Australia. This time her interest was more deeply aroused, and she shared the letter and photograph with her daughter and Meehan on a car trip through Southern California. The journey itself was rewarding; the beautiful scenery filled her with wonder. As she walked in the old mission garden at San Juan Capistrano, it occurred to her that she was in the same geographical latitude as the Holy Land. "I believe that we are seeing to-day things very like what Jesus saw when He travelled over the hills and through the valleys on His mission on earth," she noted.

On returning home, Stratton-Porter collapsed in bed. But she could not sleep. A poem began coming to her, and even though she "punched up" pillows and tried to quiet her mind, she remained too restless. "So I got up," she said, "and slipped into a heavy bathrobe and night sandals, and wrapping a big blanket around me. . . . I sat down alone in my study and wrote out the poem, as it now stands, in longhand." Stratton-Porter titled it *Jesus of the Emerald*. Later, she wrote a lengthy "Afterword" discussing the legend and her historical research. She also shared her thoughts on religion, including her belief that God had created an orderly universe and that man's salvation was part of the grand design: "In the economy of Nature nothing is ever lost. I cannot believe that the soul of man shall prove the one exception."

Doubleday, Page published *Jesus of the Emerald* in time for Christmas 1923. Gift books were popular at the time, and this "boxed" book was elaborately produced, with gilt decoration and color

drawings. Stratton-Porter, believing *Jesus of the Emerald* was the answer to her prayers that restless night, did not like leaving the rest to chance. As she had done with *The Fire Bird,* she engaged in some huckstering to boost sales. "I hope you will like the poem, and I hope you will do all in your power for its circulation among people who may need its help," she wrote to a friend. "It is the same old story: My publishers will make any kind of a beautiful book I design and send in to them, but they will not lift a finger to circulate it among the people unless it is fiction or Natural History. For poetry they have less use than a rooster would have for skates."

Opposite: A formal portrait of Stratton-Porter and her daughter, Jeannette.

10

In the summer of 1923, as Gene Stratton-Porter juggled magazine assignments, film projects, poetry writing, and speaking engagements, she savored the latest news from her publisher. Her new novel, *The White Flag*, was to be released on August 17, with the largest prepublication sale—three hundred thousand copies—of any book up to that time. "Altogether," she told a friend, "this seems to be my year."

Good Housekeeping readers were given a preview; *The White Flag* was serialized in the magazine starting in April that year—the first time Stratton-Porter had granted such permission for one of her novels. She anticipated that whatever way readers encountered her story, in magazine or in book form, they would be surprised. After years of listening to critics say she could write only "molasses fiction," she decided to switch course and write about the darker side of life. She described *The White Flag* as a "book of character analysis such as I never before have written," and she peopled it with an evil businessman, his scheming son, a demented flag bearer, and a young woman who suffers through a series of disasters. She claimed she had written a realistic novel. But reviewers strongly disagreed. One critic insisted her characters were nothing more than "stock figures in an old-fashioned melodrama." Stratton-Porter fans were decidedly unhappy, and not solely because the novel skimped on nature description. One disappointed reader spoke of hiding the book because the content was so unpleasant. Preorders aside, *The White Flag* did not live up to expectations and failed to make best-seller lists.

Too busy to brood over one novel's lackluster performance, Stratton-Porter forged ahead. New business, of a more personal nature, now occupied her attention. After several years of returning each summer to Wildflower Woods, she decided in 1923 to make California her permanent home. She wrote that autumn to Indiana governor Warren T. McCray, offering Wildflower Woods to the state: "I feel that the time has come when I am forced to ask if you will not use your influence to save this lovely place and my work upon it for the children of our state. . . . I believe the location on the lake shore could be made into a wonderful public park." Her offer came with stipulations. Stratton-Porter expected to be reimbursed for the buildings, walkways, and other improvements, as well as for the plants she brought to the site. Her secretaries had kept records over the years of every tree, shrub, bush, vine, and flower planted on the estate. "My records at the present slightly exceed 17,000 specimens which have been planted in these woods. I have also the record of every bird which has nested in the grounds and all animals habitual here." She stressed to McCray: "The collection is peculiar to Indiana, a unique thing, the like of which is not in existence in any state of the Union."

McCray referred her request to the state's conservation department, which took no action then or anytime soon. Years passed before state government finally acquired the property and opened it to the public. Meanwhile, Stratton-Porter, having committed herself to living full time in California, made plans to build two new homes. One was to be a summer retreat, the other a much larger residence-workshop.

In early 1924 Stratton-Porter bought land for her retreat, and work began on a fourteen-room house built entirely of redwood. Located on Catalina Island, about twenty-five miles by steamer from Los Angeles's harbor, the home and surroundings appealed perfectly to Stratton-Porter. "I am crazy about the mountains, the sea, and the low-hung stars; and the air is the freshest, the cleanest that I ever have had to breathe," she wrote upon moving to the island in July. At night, she listened to the bleating of wild goats on the cliffs. During the day, she spied spouting whales, bald eagles sailing overhead, and seals playing on rocks. Amid the quiet and immensities of that place, she confided in a letter that "maybe . . . I can do some bigger and better work here than I ever have done before."

Back on the mainland, work proceeded more slowly on her other residence. It sat atop a small mountain between two canyons outside Los Angeles, six miles from the ocean in an area known today as Bel Air. Plans called for twenty-two rooms, a four-car garage, and servants' quarters, with a greenhouse, tennis courts, and fish ponds located on the grounds. Charles Porter was to have his own suite consisting of a large sitting room with a fireplace, a bedroom, and a bath. The house was to have a projection room in which to show motion pictures.

Stratton-Porter instructed the architect to make sure the height of the house did not force birds to change their migration course. She also insisted that the contour and color of her home blend into the surrounding mountains. Based on her experience in Indiana, she anticipated that developers would cut down trees and strip away the region's vegetation. So she went several times a week to gather rare plants from "where they are going to make roads and destroy stuff, and move [them] over to my mountain." As she roamed her property, sowing wildflower seed and breathing in the clean smell of sage, she declared herself happy. "I so love California," she wrote a friend, "that this is the land in which I wish to finish my living and to do my dying."

But dying was the last thing on Stratton-Porter's mind that summer. She turned sixty-one in August and was feeling fit, physically and mentally. She kept up with her volumes of mail thanks to a capable new secretary named Frances Foster (Lorene Miller had married the tree surgeon Frank Wallace). She retained a loyal following of readers of her monthly *McCall's* columns and planned to write another novel, from which her new son-in-law would write the screenplay.

Stratton-Porter also remained much sought after as a speaker, especially in her fight for decency in the movies. A few months earlier, in April, she championed that cause before a packed audience of clubwomen in Los Angeles's large Philharmonic Auditorium. The ovation was thunderous. "They almost mobbed me," she wrote her sister, Florence. "I could feel women patting my back, touching my dress, and when finally my driver . . . started to drive away, at least three women were standing in the gutter with their hands thrust through the door trying to shake hands with me."

As if all that activity were not enough, she remained an important national spokesperson for protecting the environment. As a founding member in 1922 of the Izaak Walton League, a national conservation organization, Statton-Porter immediately contributed two articles to its new monthly magazine. In December that year her passionate plea for land conservation—"All Together, Heave!"—appeared on the magazine's cover. In 1924, as the league lobbied to save the starving elk of Jackson Hole, Wyoming, from extinction, she joined the campaign to raise a hundred thousand dollars for food. "I am glad to add my bit to a plea for the starving elk," she wrote in *Outdoor*

America, the league's renamed publication. But mere sympathy for that endangered wildlife near Yellowstone Park was not enough, she told readers. She urged people to take action "and do not listen any longer to my futile pen."

Meanwhile, it was physical activity, more than anything else, that occupied her time that summer of 1924. She designed an elaborate fountain for her Catalina property and, together with her driver and a Yaqui Indian, they combed the mountainous island for unusual stones. Needing more raw materials, Stratton-Porter hired a small steamer that

A view of Stratton-Porter's Bel Air mansion near Los Angeles.

her driver piloted to a small cove on the island's west side. There she gathered large seashells and brilliantly colored pebbles while the tide was out. When construction began, she labored alongside a stonemason and his assistant, dressed in her usual field garb—boots, breeches, and a floppy old Panana hat. She was happy to be stooping and lifting and getting outdoor exercise. "I know what my family says behind my back when I get out with a bunch of men and build springs and gate-posts and fireplaces and fountains," she confided to a sister. But she liked working with her hands and insisted that such experiences furnished ideas for her writing. When the fountain was finished, she listened

"What else did he blab about me?" said the little scout.

"Keeper of the bees, are you here?"

Illustrations from Stratton-Porter's last novel, *The Keeper of the Bees*, which is set in her adopted home of California and tells the story of a wounded World War I veteran restored to health through the power and beauties of nature.

with satisfaction as water trickled over each of thirty-two large shells, generating constant rippling songs. Inspired by the nature music, she named her island retreat "Singing Water."

In the fall, she was ready to resume writing. She and Foster set out each day for the hills beyond the island town of Avalon. Amid a stand of live oaks and with the sky for their roof, the two women worked. Stratton-Porter lay in a hammock, dictating two new novels and her *McCall's* columns. Foster took shorthand. "When we really work, Frances and I have learned that the thing to do is to roll up our blankets and hit it for the peace and the grandeur, for the silence of the mountains; and the higher up we get, and the quieter it is, the closer I can get to God and the big, primal, vital things of life," Stratton-Porter said.

She finished *The Keeper of the Bees*, the first of the two new novels, in record time. Having earlier written *Morning Face* for her granddaughter, Jeannette, she wrote this book for her other granddaughter, Gene Stratton Monroe. She created a character, "Little Scout," who reflected the grandchild's personality. The novel also featured a wounded war veteran—the first and only time Stratton-Porter referenced the recently concluded war in her fiction. Like her earlier work, *The Keeper of the Bees* excelled in nature description. But having already proven her in-depth knowledge of birds, moths, and flowers, this time Stratton-Porter showed she had a thorough understanding of the life history of bees.

James Leo Meehan wrote a screenplay adaptation as soon as the novel was finished. Plans called for releasing the movie version in 1925, with *McCall's* scheduled to publish the story in serial form starting in February that year. Doubleday, Page was to publish the book in August.

Another book, *Tales You Won't Believe*, was also scheduled for release in 1925. It was a collection of nature articles Stratton-Porter had earlier penned for *Good Housekeeping*.

Though she easily could have taken a break, given her stockpile of ready material, Stratton-Porter kept writing. The second novel she worked on, while still on Catalina Island, was *The Magic Garden*. It told the story of a young girl whose parents were divorced, a subject uppermost in Stratton-Porter's mind given the failure of Jeannette's first marriage. Stratton-Porter wrote *The Magic Garden,* according to Jeannette, to influence parents to stay married for the sake of their offspring and, if divorce occurred, "to remind them that both father and mother still owed a duty to the children."

In November 1924 Stratton-Porter returned to Los Angeles. Her mountain home was nearing completion, and she spent eight-hour days at the site, supervising the stonemason at work on two fireplaces. She directed where each pudding stone, shipped from Indiana, was to be placed. She had already named her baby mountain Floraves, "Flora" for flowers, "Aves" for birds, and she looked forward to moving into her Bel Air mansion in late December. In the interim, she took time off. Her daughter and son-in-law invited her to join them on a car trip to nearby Lake Arrowhead. That was followed by a car trip to San Francisco, where Stratton-Porter explored the giant redwoods of Muir Woods. At one point, Jeannette realized her mother had wandered off the path: "When we finally located her, she was so awed by the grandeur of the trees, by the odour of the thick carpet of pine needles, by the flowers and the gorgeous ferns, that she had forgotten about all time and the existence of the rest of the party."

Two days later, on December 6, 1924, Stratton-Porter left her South Serrano Avenue home in Los Angeles at about eight o'clock in the evening. Driven by her chauffeur, she planned to visit her brother Jerome, who had retired to that city. Barely a block from her house, her car collided with a streetcar. The impact threw her from the vehicle and left her unconscious. Less than two hours later, she died at a nearby hospital.

One of Stratton-Porter's last wishes, as expressed in an article she wrote for *McCall's*, was to be buried where she had most enjoyed life—in the wild: "When I am gone, I hope my family will bury me out in the open and plant a tree on my grave; I do not want a monument. A refuge for a bird nest is all the marker I want."

That last wish would not be granted in 1924. Jeannette had her mother's body temporarily interred as she waited for her father, en route by train from Indiana, to make final arrangements. Charles Porter chose not to make any changes. Stratton-Porter's body remained at the Hollywood Memorial Park Cemetery, the final resting place of many important people in the entertainment industry.

Her funeral service was December 11, a private affair conducted at her South Serrano residence. Her secretary Foster recalled how the doors were "wide open to the morning, and outside on the pergola the roses bloomed in riotous profusion and little ruby-throated hummingbirds darted from flower to flower." A church choir sang. The Reverend Benjamin S. Haywood talked at length about Stratton-Porter's contributions and her widespread influence. His opening remarks were especially fitting: "Hers was ever an original way. She did nothing after a prescribed fashion."

In the spring of 1999 Gene Stratton-Porter's remains were moved from California and buried at Wildflower Woods in a grave overlooking Sylvan Lake and surrounded by the gardens and forested paths she loved. A cluster of trees, including a magnificent chinkapin oak, provide shade for her grave. Birds nest and sing overhead.

The move was arranged by Gene Stratton-Porter's grandsons, James and John Meehan, fulfilling her wishes to be buried in her home state. James was only six months old when his grandmother died; John was born after her death. The Meehan brothers had the remains of their mother Jeannette Porter Meehan, who died in California in 1977, moved to Wildflower Woods that spring as well. Charles Porter, who died in 1926, was buried in his hometown of Decatur, Indiana.

In the 1940s the Gene Stratton-Porter Memorial Association purchased Wildflower Woods from Jeannette, who was her mother's sole heir. In 1946 the association donated the property to the State of Indiana, which today operates it as the Gene Stratton-Porter State Historic Site. Her other Indiana home, the Limberlost Cabin in Geneva, was acquired by the state in 1947. It, too, is operated as a state historic site. Both of her former homes attract thousands of visitors each year.

In the latter years of her life, Stratton-Porter had effectively used mass-market magazines and motion pictures—the new media tools of that era—to spread her nature-infused message of hard work and clean living. That same media, for a period, served her well after her death. She had developed the habit of writing her magazine columns far in advance of deadlines. As a result, *McCall's* had enough material on hand that it published "Gene Stratton-Porter's Page" monthly through December 1927, a full three years after she died. *Good Housekeeping* and *American Magazine* also published articles by her posthumously. Such was also the case with her books. *Tales You Won't Believe*, the collection of her nature articles from *Good Housekeeping*, appeared in April 1925; *The Keeper of the Bees* came out in August that year. *The Magic Garden*, the last of her novels, was published in 1927. Doubt remains as to whether Stratton-Porter actually completed this work, given its lack of polish and shortness; daughter Jeannette or someone else may have finished it. In 1927 one other, final, Stratton-Porter book was published; *Let Us Highly Resolve* is a collection of her essays that had previously appeared in *McCall's*.

Son-in-law James Leo Meehan continued to operate Gene Stratton-Porter Productions and to direct the silent-film versions of her novels after her death. *The Keeper of the Bees* was released in 1925, followed by *Laddie* (1926), *The Magic Garden* (1927), *The Harvester* (1927), and *Freckles* (1928). Filming of *The Harvester* took place at Wildflower Woods in the spring of 1927, with the Meehans and a sizable cast and crew present at Sylvan Lake.

By the decade's end, the filmmaking business underwent a dramatic change as "talking" movies became all the rage. Adding sound to movies was costly. Gene Stratton-Porter Productions went out of business in the late 1920s. Even so, Stratton-Porter's popular stories continued to interest filmmakers. "Talking" movies based on her books were produced by a number of companies in the 1930s and 1940s. *Freckles* was produced multiple times, as recently as 1960 by Twentieth-Century Fox and again in 1993 for public television. *A Girl of the Limberlost* also was remade several times, most recently in 1990. In all, eight of her novels were made into movies.

Exterior view of Stratton-Porter's home at Rome City, the Cabin at Wildflower Woods, today a state historic site under the auspices of the Indiana State Museum system.

Stratton-Porter's fictional works, though not read nearly as much as they once were, still appeal to people who like sentiment and romance. Indiana University Press reissued eight of her novels during the 1980s and 1990s. *A Girl of the Limberlost* remains among her best-loved novels, and on the occasion of its centennial anniversary in 2009, a writer in *The New York Review of Books* called it Stratton-Porter's best book—one that had secured "a special place . . . in American popular art."

Her nature books, meanwhile, did not show as much staying power after her death; most were relegated to storage in library basements.

A panoramic view of the scenery at the Cabin at Wildflower Woods.

They have begun, however, to gain fresh attention. A book examining her role as a serious chronicler of the outdoors, and filled with her nature essays, appeared in the late 1990s. Stratton-Porter's essay, "The Last Passenger Pigeon," earned a place in an anthology, published in 2008, of the most significant environmental writing from the past two centuries. Even her poetry is undergoing scholarly reappraisal. In 2007 Kent State University Press published a first-ever collection of her poems. The introductory chapter discusses how Stratton-Porter matured as a poet and how her poems, taken together, displayed "a growing and astonishing range of form as well as of topic and tone."

The Limberlost, that watery and forested region that served to launch Stratton-Porter's writing career, is also making something

of a comeback. Through a project known as Limberlost Swamp Remembered, portions of the former swamp are being restored to a wild state. Beginning in the 1990s, conservation-minded citizens—many directly inspired by her books—encouraged landowners to convert farm acreage to wetlands and to create nature preserves. Hundreds of waterfowl—mallards, bufflehead, green-winged teal, mergansers, and wood ducks—have returned to the restored marshes. Plants not seen for years also have taken root; the fringes of shallow ponds display thick growths of cattails, bulrushes, swamp milkweed, sedges, bur reed, ironweed, and native grasses. Visitors hiking through the area can now enjoy some of the natural wonders that Stratton-Porter once photographed and described. "The Limberlost stirred," she

The Limberlost Cabin in Geneva is also operated as a state historic site. The home features some original pieces, including bedroom furniture by the Grand Rapids Furniture Company of Michigan.

wrote in 1904 in her best-selling novel *Freckles*. Today, in a remnant of Limberlost country, conservationists celebrate the land's wild stirrings once again.

Today, too, Hoosiers are finding, and will likely continue to find, new ways to honor their native daughter. In 2009 a Stratton-Porter portrait was added to the Hoosier Heritage Portrait Collection in the Governor's Office at the Indiana Statehouse in Indianapolis. That same year she also was posthumously inducted into the charter class of the Indiana Conservation Hall of Fame. Stratton-Porter and the other inductees were saluted for their efforts to preserve the state's "irreplaceable treasures."

Stratton-Porter undoubtedly would have appreciated the tributes; she liked to be recognized. But it was a deeply felt concern for the environment, more than a desire for others' esteem, that propelled her to champion wildlife and wild places. As she demonstrated throughout her career, and as she noted in 1916, "the task I set myself was to lead every human being I could influence afield; but with such reverence instilled into their touch that devastation would not be ultimately complete."

Freckles (1904)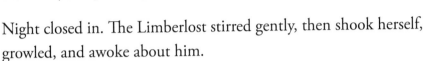

Night closed in. The Limberlost stirred gently, then shook herself, growled, and awoke about him.

There seemed to be a great owl hooting from every hollow tree and a little one screeching from every knothole. The bellowing of monster bullfrogs was not sufficiently deafening to shut out the wailing of whip-poor-wills that seemed to come from every bush. Night-hawks swept past him with their shivering cry, and bats struck his face. A prowling wildcat missed its catch and screamed with rage. A lost fox bayed incessantly for its mate.

The hair on the back of Freckles' neck rose like bristles, and his knees wavered beneath him. He could not see if the dreaded snakes were on the trail, nor, in the pandemonium, hear the rattle for which McLean had cautioned him to listen. He stood rooted to the ground in an agony of fear. His breath whistled between his teeth. The perspiration ran down his face and body in little streams.

A Girl of the Limberlost (1909)

"Elnora Comstock, have you lost your senses?" demanded the angry voice of Katharine Comstock while she glared at her daughter.

"Why, mother!" faltered the girl.

"Don't you 'why, mother' me!" cried Mrs. Comstock. "You know very well what I mean. You've given me no peace until you've had your way about this going to school business; I've fixed you good enough, and you're ready to start. But no child of mine walks the streets of Onabasha looking like a play-actress woman. You wet your hair and comb it down modest and decent and then be off, or you'll have no time to find where you belong."

Elnora gave one despairing glance at the white face, framed in a most becoming riot of reddish-brown hair, which she saw in the little kitchen mirror. Then she untied the narrow black ribbon, wet the comb and plastered the waving curls close to her head, bound them fast, pinned on the skimpy black hat and opened the back door.

"You've gone so plum daffy you are forgetting your dinner," jeered her mother.

"I don't want anything to eat," replied Elnora.

"You'll take your dinner or you'll not go one step. Are you crazy? Walk nearly three miles and no food from six in the morning until six at night. A pretty figure you'd cut if you had your way! And after I've gone and bought you this nice new pail and filled it especial to start on!"

Elnora came back with a face still whiter and picked up the lunch. "Thank you, mother! Good-bye!" she said. Mrs. Comstock did not reply. She watched the girl down the long walk to the gate and go from sight on the road, in the bright sunshine of the first Monday of September.

"I bet a dollar she gets enough of it by night!" commented Mrs. Comstock.

Elnora walked by instinct, for her eyes were blinded with tears. She left the road where it turned south at the corner of the Limberlost, climbed a snake fence and entered a path worn by her own feet. Dodging under willow and scrub oak branches she came at last to the faint outline of an old trail made in the days when the precious timber of the swamp was guarded by armed men. This path she followed until she reached a thick clump of bushes. From the debris in the end of a hollow log she took a key that unlocked the padlock of a large weather-beaten old box, inside of which lay several books, a butterfly apparatus, and a small cracked mirror. The walls were lined thickly with gaudy butterflies, dragonflies, and moths. She set up the mirror, and once more pulling the ribbon from her hair, she shook the bright mass over her shoulders, tossing it dry in the sunshine. Then she straightened it, bound it loosely, and replaced her hat. She tugged vainly at the low brown calico collar and gazed despairingly at the generous length of the narrow skirt. She lifted it as she would have cut it if possible. That disclosed the heavy high leather shoes, at sight of which she looked positively ill, and hastily dropped the skirt. She opened the pail, removed the lunch, wrapped it in the napkin, and placed it in a small pasteboard box. Locking the case again she hid the key and hurried down the trail.

She followed it around the north end of the swamp and then entered a footpath crossing a farm leading in the direction of the spires of the city to the northeast. Again she climbed a fence and was on the open road. For an instant she leaned against the fence staring before her, then turned and looked back. Behind her lay the land on which she had been born to drudgery and a mother who made no pretence of loving her; before her lay the city through whose schools she hoped to find means of escape and the way to reach the things for which she cared. When she thought of how she appeared she leaned more heavily against the fence and groaned; when she thought of turning back and wearing such clothing in ignorance all the days of her life, she set her teeth firmly and went hastily toward Onabasha.

Music of the Wild (1910)

It was Thoreau who, in writing of the destruction of the forests, exclaimed, "Thank Heaven, they can not cut down the clouds!" Aye, but they can! That is a miserable fact, and soon it will become our discomfort and loss. Clouds are beds of vapor arising from damp places and floating in air until they meet other vapor masses, that mingle with them, and the weight becomes so great the whole falls in drops of rain. If men in their greed cut forests that preserve and distil moisture, clear fields, take the shelter of trees from creeks and rivers until they evaporate, and drain the water from swamps so that they can be cleared and cultivated, —they *prevent vapor from rising*; and if it does not rise it can not fall. Pity of pities it is; but man can change and is changing the forces of nature. I never told a sadder truth, but it is truth that man can "cut down the clouds."

Moths of the Limberlost (1912)

In the selection of [Cecropia] cocoons, hold them to the ear, and with a quick motion reverse them end for end. If there is a dull, solid thump, the moth is alive, and will emerge all right. If this thump is lacking, and there is a rattle like a small seed shaking in a dry pod, it means that the caterpillar has gone into the cocoon with one of the tiny parasites that infest these worms, clinging to it, and the pupa has been eaten by the parasite.

In fall and late summer are the best times to find cocoons, as birds tear open many of them in winter; and when weather-beaten they fade, and do not show the exquisite shadings of silk of those newly spun.

When fresh, the colours range from almost white through lightest tans and browns to a genuine red, and there is a silvery effect that is lovely on some of the large, baggy ones, hidden under bridges. Out of doors the moths emerge in middle May or June, but they are earlier in the heat of a house. They are the largest of any species, and exquisitely coloured, the shades being strongest on the upper side of the wings. They differ greatly in size, most males having an average wing sweep of five inches, and a female that emerged in my conservatory from a cocoon that I wintered with particular care had a spread of seven inches, the widest of which I have heard; six and three quarters is a large female. The moth, on appearing, seems all head and abdomen, the wings hanging limp and wet from the shoulders. It at once creeps around until a place where it can hang with the wings down is found, and soon there begins a sort of pumping motion of the body. I imagine this is to start circulation, to exercise parts, and force blood into the wings. They begin to expand, to dry, to take on colour with amazing rapidity, and as soon as they are full size and crisp, the moth commences raising and lowering them slowly, as in flight. If a male, he emerges near ten in the forenoon, and flies at dusk in search of a mate.

Laddie: A True Blue Story (1913)

Schoolhouses are made wrong. If they must be, they should be built in a woods pasture beside a stream, where you could wade, swim, and be comfortable in summer, and slide and skate in winter. The windows should be cut to the floor, and stand wide open, so the birds and butterflies could pass through. You ought to learn your geography by climbing a hill, walking through a valley, wading creeks, making islands in them, and promontories, capes, and peninsulas along the bank. You should do your arithmetic sitting under trees adding hickorynuts, subtracting walnuts, multiplying butternuts, and dividing hazelnuts. You could use apples for fractions, and tin cups for liquid measure. You could spell everything in sight and this would teach you the words that are really used in the world.

"The Barn Owl" from *Morning Face* (1916)

When weary work horses are stabled,

When sleeping lie cattle and sheep,

  When the rat's tooth grates in the silence,

From my dark, warm tree I creep;

  I fly to white doves on the rafters,

To chickens on the stalls below,

Make my feast upon the choicest,

  Then awaken you jeering as I go:

"Hoo, hoo, hoo, hoot! Hoo, hoo, hoo, hoot!

  Read the story in feathers white,

To-whit, to-hoot! Hoo, hoo, hoo, hoot!

  I'll call again to-morrow night.

Homing with the Birds (1919)

I had my camera focused on the nest of a pair of kingbirds to which both of the old birds were coming constantly, each by a private route, to feed the young. The male at each approach to the nest flew to the end of a twig on which the nest was located. This branch was alive and small apples were sticking up around the nest, but the extreme tip, on which the bird alighted from a higher point in his route, was dead and bare so that every natural history point possible to include in one picture was shown almost every time he alighted. Noticing this, I decided to move the camera a few feet, focus it on the tip of the branch, and see if I could secure a picture of him during the instant he perched there before he flew to the nest. After he had left from one feeding I moved the camera, made the focus as sharp as possible, and retired to hiding. The picture I secured was made the first time he alighted on the twig. As he struck it, he noticed the camera was in a different position. He drew back his head, but did not move his body. The picture shows him breast toward the camera, his head slightly turned to one side, which resulted in giving the exact shape of his beak, his eye, the height and rounding of his crest, his wings not tightly folded to his sides, his feet both in view as they naturally grasped the twig, his tail widespread showing the white border, his pose alert. I scarcely see how it would be possible to crowd more interesting points into one reproduction of a bird, while on his face is plainly to be seen the curiosity he undoubtedly was experiencing as to what the camera was, and why the strange object had moved since his latest trip to the nest.

Front cover editorial for *The Izaak Walton League Monthly* (later renamed *Outdoor America*), December 1922

Today we are squarely facing the problem of reparation, for we must make reparation or we must meet disaster. . . . If we do not want our land to dry up and blow away, we must replace at least part of our lost trees. We must save every brook and stream and lake. . . . The case is imperative; the work necessary to protect, to preserve, to propagate natural resources for the future is up to every one of us. . . . It no longer becomes a question of what we want to do. We are now facing a fair and square presentment of what we must do, and those of us who see the vision and most keenly feel the need must furnish the motor power for those less responsive. Work must be done. It is the time for all of us to get together and in unison make a test of our strength. All together, Heave!

Undated letter, circa 1924, describing her new home in California to an unidentified acquaintance, from *The Lady of the Limberlost: The Life and Letters of Gene Stratton-Porter* **by Jeannette Porter Meehan**

I cannot remember whether I told you of buying five acres of land out in the hills about six miles from the ocean on a little baby mountain half-way down the side of the range with a highly interesting growth of native timber and flowers on it. On the mountain I am going to set my workshop, fashioned much like Limberlost Cabin in size and arrangement, but differing from it in architecture as it must conform to this location; and around it I am going to begin growing the wild flowers of California. I want it, also, as I want any spot on which I live, to become a sanctuary for the birds....

I got keen joy yesterday out of ploughing up perhaps half an acre at the foot of the mountain, having it harrowed, and sowing it in wildflower seed. While I was doing this I made the acquaintance of a California jay which is certainly a brilliant bird, and a pair of brown velvet thrushes who followed down the rows and ate wildflower seed about as fast as I could sow it. And I also had the pleasure of leaving inviolate the home of Mr. and Mrs. Trade Rat, and I advanced some way in forming an acquaintance with them. I observed that they have rounder noses, shorter, broader tails, and are larger than our Eastern rats, and they have a very docile, friendly disposition. It seems that they steal every bright thing they can lay their teeth on, but they never take anything without making a return gift. The entrance to their tunnel is covered with a mass of wild stuff as big around as a washtub and two or three feet in height. It is an interesting collection of weed stems, little sticks, reeds, long bright grasses, yucca seeds, the lace of wild cucumber seed pods, nut shells, acorns, bits of wire and string, bright pebbles, anything and everything, all heaped up in a most interesting manner.

I often take my work out to the location where there is the loveliest canyon that I ever have seen in all my life, bar none. My driver has made me a table and benches out of rough boards and Frances and I work there in the open with the birds and the wildflowers all about us and the clean smell of the sage in our nostrils. I am more deeply convinced than ever that this is the only place I have seen in California where I really wanted to build a home, a place so exactly suited to the requirements of the work I dream of doing there; and I have long since decided that I so love California that this is the land in which I wish to finish my living and to do my dying.

"Do We Waste Time?" published posthumously in *McCall's*, January 1927, collected in *Let Us Highly Resolve* (1927)

People complain continually because they have not time to do so-and-so. The answer is that we *do* have the time, it is God-given, twenty-four precious hours each day, and it is ours to do with as we please. It is strictly our own affair what we do with it; it is to be hoped that each individual strives to better himself and to help his neighbour.…

All right, then. We must spend our spare moments thinking; we must not waste them in idle gazing into space. Dreaming is all right if we make the dreams come true, but too many of us just dream, and the reality never comes. Do you think while you are riding, while you are walking, while you are sewing, while you are playing golf, while you are washing, and while you are taking a bath, while you are on your way to work, and while you are rocking the baby to sleep? I once outlined a short story, for which I was paid a good price, while I was in a beauty parlour having my hair shampooed. This is what I mean by the time we waste; the time that our bodies may be relaxed and resting is the best time in the world for our brains to be active. There is sufficient time wasted in gossip and idle chatter in beauty parlours alone to evolve plans for saving a whole heaven full of souls, or for making fortunes in dollars or in friendship.…

I was once asked to write a list of the events in any one day of my life, which was to stand as typical of all the other days. This I found impossible. Some days I am a natural historian afield hunting rare flowers. Some days I am an amateur photographer, hidden among the bushes with a camera trained on a bird nest. Some days I am high up in the mountains dictating book material or magazine articles to my secretary. Some days I am on a raft on the ocean gathering stone when the tide is out. Some days I am working with stone masons making drinking fountains or seed trays for the birds, or setting up mantels of "pudden" stone for my home. Some days I am on my hands and knees transplanting rare wild flowers. Some days I am dressing dolls for little crippled children. Some days I am criticizing manuscripts for struggling youngsters who are trying to write. Some days I am painting moths to illustrate a book. Some days I play with my grandchildren, and go on picnics with my family or friends. Life turns a page every morning and opens up busy days for me; and I am glad, for I cannot be happy unless I am occupied with something useful. And I hope fervently that each of you has something to do, or, if you have not, then I hope you will look about and hunt something to occupy your brain and your hands. There is nothing more pathetic and pitiful than the individual who has "nothing to do." There is so much to be done!

Undated letter to Miss Hazel Allen, Los Angeles, from *The Lady of the Limberlost*

Certainly I try with all my might to keep my life straight in the sight of my Creator and to do as I would be done by in my dealings with my neighbours . . . . I am not a member of any church, not because I do not believe in creeds and churches for the great majority of people, but because in my personal case I have the feeling that they are not necessary. I prefer to continue in the relationship I feel is established between me and my Creator through a lifetime of Nature study.

The following sites will lead the reader to a broader understanding of some of the most important experiences in Gene Stratton-Porter's life. If you plan on making a visit to one of these places, please call, write, or visit its website for the most up-to-date information.

The "Limberlost Cabin" is now the **Limberlost State Historic Site**. It is located at 200 East Sixth Street, one block east of US 27, in Geneva, Indiana. Stratton-Porter's fourteen-room home was given to the State of Indiana in 1947 by the Limberlost Conservation Association of Geneva. Today the home is operated by the Indiana State Museum and Historic Sites.

The Wisconsin cedar-log cabin, which Stratton-Porter helped design, includes three rooms paneled in red oak: the entrance hall, dining room, and library. Elsewhere on the first floor visitors can tour the conservatory, music room, two bedrooms, and the kitchen, which has been converted into a gift shop. Stratton-Porter's memorabilia, furniture, and paintings are on display, including a moth collection she mounted in 1906. The carriage house has been converted to a Wetland Education Center, where visitors can learn about the natural history of nearby marshlands—once home to the swamp Stratton-Porter made famous in her writings.

Guided tours of the cabin are conducted year-round and group tours are available by appointment. Admission is $3.50 for adults, $3 for seniors, and $2 for children ages four to eleven. The site is open from 9 a.m. to 5 p.m. Wednesday through Saturday, and 1 p.m. to 5 p.m. on Sunday. Winter hours may vary. For more information and

hours of operation, call the site at (260) 368-7428 or visit its Web site
at http://www.indianamuseum.org/sites/limb.html.

The **Loblolly Marsh Wetland Preserve** is west and south of the
Limberlost State Historic Site in Adams County and neighboring
Jay County. Located in a portion of the former Limberlost Swamp,
the Loblolly Marsh consists of 442 acres restored to wetlands and
maintained by the state Division of Nature Preserves. Guided walking
tours through the marsh are offered June through September on the
first Saturday of the month. The cost is $2 per person. Orientation
begins at 9:30 a.m. at the Limberlost Cabin, with a tour from 10 a.m.
to noon. For more information, contact the Limberlost State Historic
Site at (260) 368-7428 or e-mail limberlostshs@dnr.in.gov.

Geneva Area Nature Attractions: Near the Limberlost Cabin
are sites that inspired Stratton-Porter's writings and where she went

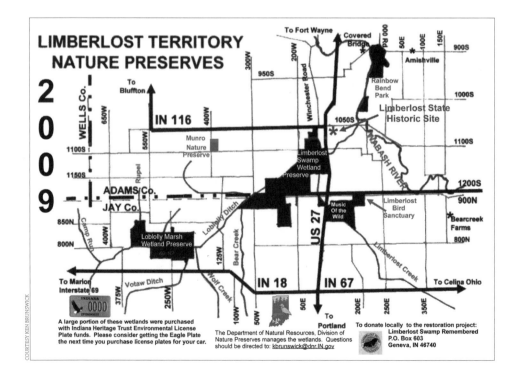

regularly to do fieldwork. These include the thirty-eight-acre Limberlost Bird Sanctuary (walking trail through woods), the sixty-seven-acre "Music of the Wild" prairie and woods (limited hiking area), Rainbow Bend Park on the Wabash River (hiking trails, views of river), and the Limberlost Swamp Wetland Preserve, an 840-acre swath of land that, like the Loblolly, is being restored to its former marshy state (drive-by views). Also nearby is the Munro Nature Preserve, owned by ACRES Land Trust. A half-mile loop trail, with trees identified, winds through the twenty-five-acre preserve. The remains of the old Brushwood School, mentioned in *A Girl of the Limberlost*, can be seen at this site. For more information, visit the Division of Nature Preserves online at http://www.in.gov/dnr/naturepreserve/ or ACRES Land Trust at http://www.acreslandtrust.org/.

The **Gene Stratton-Porter State Historic Site** is located on the southern shores of Sylvan Lake near Rome City, Indiana. It encompasses 125 acres, twenty of which were part of her original Wildflower Woods estate. Still intact from when Stratton-Porter lived there are the formal gardens and wooded paths, along with the spacious cabin she designed. The State acquired the property in 1946, and it is operated today by the Indiana State Museum and Historic Sites.

Like Stratton-Porter's home in Geneva, this two-story cabin has a cedar-log exterior and a large front porch. The entrance hall and dining room are paneled in wild cherry harvested from the site. Notable features include a photographic darkroom, a large picture window that afforded her awe-inspiring views of the lake, and a living-room fireplace imbedded with Native American artifacts collected by Charles Porter on his trips to Central America. Many of Stratton-Porter's furnishings and memorabilia are on display, including her personal library, donated by her daughter, Jeannette Porter Meehan.

Wildflower Woods is located five miles west of Kendallville on US 6 and three miles north on Indiana 9. Follow the signs. Guided tours of the cabin are conducted April 1 through December 1. The cabin is open from 10 a.m. to 5 p.m. Tuesday through Saturday, and from 1 p.m. to 5 p.m. on Sunday, with the last tour starting each day at 4 p.m. Group tours are available in the winter by appointment. A visitor center, replicating the old carriage house that was destroyed by fire in the 1920s, houses a gift shop, meeting rooms, and exhibitions on Stratton-Porter's life and work. The grounds, with trails and picnic facilities, are open dawn to dusk year-round. Admission for cabin tours is $3.50 for adults, $3 for seniors, and $2 for children ages six to twelve. For more information and hours of operation, call the museum at (260) 854-3790 or visit its Web site at http://www.indianamuseum .org/sites/gene.html.

Gene Stratton-Porter's childhood home on Hopewell Farm in Wabash County no longer stands. But the brick Hopewell Methodist Episcopal Church that her father allowed to be built on the farm and where he preached, still remains, as does the adjoining cemetery. Numerous members of Stratton-Porter's family are buried there, including her parents and her beloved brother Leander (Laddie). At one point, Stratton-Porter considered buying back the family farm, restoring the property, and retiring there. However, the house had been burned, her mother's trees were gone, creeks had been filled in, and most of the forest had been cut. "All my love and ten times the money . . . never could have put back the face of nature as I knew it on that land," she later wrote.

Today the Hopewell Cemetery Board owns the former church building, which is open only rarely. The building and public cemetery are located at the intersection of County Roads 300 North and 500

East, northeast of Lagro, Indiana. Selected items within the church
were donated to the Wabash County Historical Museum, which has a
small display about Stratton-Porter. The museum also has information
and artifacts detailing post-Civil War life in the city of Wabash, where
Stratton-Porter moved after leaving Hopewell Farm. The museum
is located at 36 East Market Street, Wabash. For more information,
contact the museum at (260) 563-9070 or visit its Web site at
http://www.wabashmuseum.org/.

LEARN MORE ABOUT
GENE STRATTON-PORTER

Many libraries house a sizable collection of books by and about Gene Stratton-Porter. Of special note are: the Indiana State Library and the Indiana Historical Society's William Henry Smith Memorial Library in Indianapolis, the Lilly Library at Indiana University in Bloomington, the Cunningham Memorial Library at Indiana State University in Terre Haute, the Allen County Public Library in Fort Wayne, the Wabash Carnegie Public Library in Wabash, and the Geneva branch of the Adams Public Library in Geneva.

The Indiana State Museum in Indianapolis has an extensive collection of Stratton-Porter's nature photographs, some images of her and her family, and movie stills from *Laddie* and *Michael O'Halloran*. The Geneva branch of the Adams Public Library and the IHS library also have photographs of her and taken by her.

The Geneva branch library, the Lilly Library, the ISM, and the Bracken Library at Ball State University have some of Stratton-Porter's personal correspondence, as does the Buffalo and Erie County Historical Society Archives in Buffalo, New York. The Wabash Carnegie Public Library has a few letters written by Stratton-Porter's daughter, Jeannette Porter Meehan.

The ISM has other miscellaneous material, including postcards of her Wildflower Woods estate and Limberlost, her magazine articles, and posters from her movies. Numerous libraries have newspaper clipping files on Stratton-Porter, including the Limberlost branch of the Kendallville Public Library in Rome City, which also has a display of her first-edition books. The Kendallville Public Library in Kendallville has a scrapbook collection of M. F. Owen, a prominent Rome City businessman. The collection includes clippings about Stratton-Porter's activities at Sylvan Lake.

Stratton-Porter always guarded her privacy and was highly selective about personal information that she shared with readers. In 1914 she presented her version of her family history in Clarkson Weesner's *History of Wabash County* (Chicago: Lewis Publishing Company, 1914). A year later, she supplied an autobiographical sketch that her publisher released in a booklet titled *Gene Stratton-Porter: A Little Story of the Life and Work and Ideals of "The Bird Woman"* (Garden City, NY: Doubleday, Page and Company, 1915). The compiler of the volume was listed only by the initials S. F. E. (attributed to both Eugene Francis Saxton and Samuel F. Ewart). At the time of the booklet's release, Doubleday, Page reported that it had been receiving repeated requests for information about her and that her nature work and Limberlost stories had "stirred much curiosity among readers everywhere." As her career progressed, Stratton-Porter provided additional autobiographical material, especially in the opening chapters of her nature book *Homing with the Birds* (1919), and in articles for *McCall's, Good Housekeeping, Ladies' Home Journal,* and other publications. She always claimed that her novel *Laddie* (1913) was a faithful representation of her childhood on Hopewell Farm: "I could write no truer biography."

After Stratton-Porter's death, Jeannette reminisced about her mother in *The Lady of the Limberlost: The Life and Letters of Gene Stratton-Porter* (Garden City, NY: Doubleday, Doran and Company, 1928). Much later, other biographies appeared. Rollin Patterson King wrote admiringly of her in *Gene Stratton-Porter: A Lovely Light* (Chicago: Adams Press, 1979). A year later, Bertrand F. Richards assessed her career in *Gene Stratton-Porter: A Literary Examination*

(Boston: Twayne Publishers, 1980), part of Twayne's United States Authors Series. A decade later, Judith Reick Long wrote the most in-depth biography to date: *Gene Stratton-Porter: Novelist and Naturalist* (Indianapolis: Indiana Historical Society, 1990). This book places the novelist/naturalist in a less flattering light, with Long arguing that Stratton-Porter's autobiographical writings often were misleading, particularly with regard to her family history and early home life.

More recently, Stratton-Porter's life was summarized and her nature studies were examined in *Coming through the Swamp: The Nature Writings of Gene Stratton Porter*, edited by Sydney Landon Plum (Salt Lake City: University of Utah Press, 1996). More recently, too, a brief biography accompanied a compilation of her poetry in *Field o' My Dreams: The Poetry of Gene Stratton-Porter*, edited by Mary DeJong Obuchowski (Kent, OH: Kent State University Press, 2007).

Stratton-Porter's life was also examined in the award-winning documentary *Gene Stratton-Porter: Voice of the Limberlost*, produced by Ann Eldridge and Nancy Carlson (a coproduction of Ball State University and Indiana University Press, 1996). Another videorecording, *A Walk in the Woods with Gene Stratton-Porter* (Salt Lake City, Utah: Bonneville Worldwide Entertainment, 1998, produced by Ann Eldridge), discussed her love for wildlife and her contributions to preserving forests and marshlands.

Ball State University maintains an extensive website on the life and work of Stratton-Porter and the Limberlost region. See "Our Land, Our Literature—Gene Stratton-Porter" Ball State University (http://www.bsu.edu/ourlandourlit/literature/authors/portergs.htm).

Books and Articles

Bailey, Flossie Enyart. *Pioneer Days in the Wabash Valley: With a Review of the Life of Gene Stratton Porter.* Logansport, IN: Hendricks Brothers Company, 1933.

Banta, Richard E., ed. *Hoosier Caravan: A Treasury of Indiana Life and Lore.* Bloomington: Indiana University Press, 1975.

Boomhower, Ray E. *The Country Contributor: The Life and Times of Juliet V. Strauss.* Carmel: Guild Press of Indiana, 1998 See chapter 4 for information on *Ladies' Home Journal* editor Edward W. Bok.

"A Brave Girl." *New York Times Book Review* (August 21, 1909).

Bussell, John Chase. *The Technique of Gene Stratton-Porter's Novels.* Decatur, IN: Americana Books, 1993.

Cooper, Frederic Taber. "The Popularity of Gene Stratton-Porter." *The Bookman* (August 1915).

The Country Life Press. Garden City, NY: Doubleday, Page and Company, 1919. Published for the friends of Doubleday, Page and Company.

Dahlke-Scott, Deborah, and Michael Prewitt. "A Writer's Crusade to Portray Spirit of the Limberlost." *Smithsonian* (April 1976).

Finney, Jan Dearmin. *Gene Stratton-Porter: The Natural Wonder.* Mattituck, NY: Amereon, 1983.

"Gene Stratton-Porter." *The Indiana Historian* (September 1996).

Gene Stratton-Porter: Author and Naturalist. Booklet, Indiana State Museum and Historic Sites (November 1984, revised April 1994).

"Gene Stratton-Porter—Passes On." *Outdoor America* (January 1925).

Gorman, Herbert S. "Ingrowing Ecstasy." *The Bookman* (September 1922).

Grayson, Eric. "Limberlost Found: Indiana's Literary Legacy in Hollywood." *Traces of Indiana and Midwestern History* (Winter 2007).

Hackett, Alice P. *70 Years of Best Sellers, 1895–1965.* New York: R. R. Bowker Company, 1967.

Hamilton, Suzan Lawson, ed. *The History of Lagro.* Lagro, IN: Commercial Printing of Lagro, 2000.

Hunt, Caroline C., ed. "Gene Stratton-Porter." In *Four Women Writers for Children, 1868–1918.* Detroit: Gale Research Company, 1996.

"In Memoriam Gene Stratton-Porter." *McCall's* (February 1925).

MacLean, David G. *Gene Stratton-Porter: Bibliography and Collector's Guide.* Decatur, IN: Americana Books, 1976.

———, ed. *Gene Stratton-Porter Remembered . . . Reprints of Selected Articles, Series 1–6.* Decatur, IN: Americana Books, 1987, 1990.

Malcolm, Janet. "Capitalist Pastorale." *The New York Review of Books* (January 15, 2009).

McKibben, Bill, ed. *American Earth: Environmental Writing since Thoreau.* New York: Library of America, 2008.

Memorial Service for Gene Stratton-Porter. Warsaw, IN: Bradway Enterprises, 1990.

Morrow, Barbara Olenyik. *From Ben-Hur to Sister Carrie: Remembering the Lives and Works of Five Indiana Authors.* Indianapolis: Guild Press of Indiana, 1995.

Mott, Frank Luther. *Golden Multitudes: The Story of Best Sellers in the United States.* New York: R. R. Bowker Company, 1947.

Nye, Russel. *The Unembarrassed Muse: The Popular Arts in America.* New York: The Dial Press, 1970.

Overton, Grant Martin. "Naturalist vs. Novelist: Gene Stratton-Porter." In *American Nights Entertainment.* New York: D. Appleton and Company, 1923.

Phelps, William Lyon. "The Why of the Best Seller." *The Bookman* (December 1921).

Purcell, Denise. "Limberlost Recreated." *Outdoor Indiana* (July/August 1999).

Review of *A Girl of the Limberlost. Booklist* (October 1909).

Review of *Laddie. The New York Times* (September 7, 1913).

Review of *Laddie. Athenaeum* (September 27, 1913).

Review of *Michael O'Halloran. The Nation* (August 26, 1915).

Review of *Music of the Wild. The Nation* (May 18, 1911).

Sanders, Scott Russell. "Limberlost and Found." *Audubon* (May–June 2001).

Shumaker, Arthur W. *A History of Indiana Literature.* Indianapolis: Indiana Historical Bureau, 1962.

"Some Books on Botany and Gardening." *The Spectator* (September 9, 1911).

"The Timber-Guard's Paradise." *New York Times Book Review* (December 3, 1904).

Vanausdall, Jeanette. *Pride and Protest: The Novel in Indiana.* Indianapolis: Indiana Historical Society, 1999.

Wallace, Mrs. Frank [Lorene]. "Snowbound at Limberlost Cabin." *Indianapolis Star*, February 25, 1940.

Weber, Ronald. *The Midwestern Ascendancy in American Writing.* Bloomington and Indianapolis: Indiana University Press, 1992.

Gene Stratton-Porter and Related Web sites

"Jean-Henri Fabre: 1823–1915" http://www.museum.unl.edu/research/entomology/workers/JFabre.htm.

"The History of Doubleday" http://www.randomhouse.com/doubleday/history.

"Indiana's Popular History: Gene Stratton Porter" Indiana Historical Society http://indianahistory.org/pop_hist/people/gs_porter.html.

"The Influenza Pandemic of 1918" http://virus.stanford.edu/uda/.

"The Izaak Walton League of America" http://www.iwla.org/.

"Life of Theodore Roosevelt"
Theodore Roosevelt Association
http://www.theodoreroosevelt.org/life/lifeoftr.htm.

"The Life and Work of Gene Stratton-Porter"
Wabash Carnegie Public Library
http://www.wabash.lib.in.us/porter.html.

"The Loblolly Nature Trail"
Loblolly Marsh and Wetland Preserve Virtual Nature Trail
http://www.bsu.edu/web/landandlit/special_projects/loblolly/draft/.

"The National Parks: America's Best Idea"
A Film by Ken Burns, six-episode series coproduced by Florentine
Films and WETA, Washington, D.C., for the Public Broadcasting
System
http://www.pbs.org/nationalparks.

Gene Stratton-Porter's Novels (by date of publication)

The Song of the Cardinal. Indianapolis: Bobbs-Merrill, 1903.

Freckles. New York: Doubleday, Page and Company, 1904.

At the Foot of the Rainbow. New York: The Outing Publishing
Company, 1907.

A Girl of the Limberlost. New York: Doubleday, Page and Company,
1909.

The Harvester. Garden City, NY: Doubleday, Page and Company, 1911.

Laddie. Garden City, NY: Doubleday, Page and Company, 1913.

Michael O'Halloran. Garden City, NY: Doubleday, Page and Company, 1915.

A Daughter of the Land. Garden City, NY: Doubleday, Page and Company, 1918.

Her Father's Daughter. Garden City, NY: Doubleday, Page and Company, 1921.

The White Flag. Garden City, NY: Doubleday, Page and Company, 1923. Serialization in *Good Housekeeping* April through November 1923.

The Keeper of the Bees. Garden City, NY: Doubleday, Page and Company, 1925. Serialization in *McCall's* February through September 1925.

The Magic Garden. Garden City, NY: Doubleday, Page and Company, 1927. Serialization in *McCall's* October 1926 through March 1927.

Gene Stratton-Porter's Nature Books (by date of publication)

What I Have Done with Birds. Indianapolis: Bobbs-Merrill, 1907.

Birds of the Bible. Cincinnati: Jennings and Graham, 1909.

Music of the Wild. Cincinnati: Jennings and Graham, 1910.

Moths of the Limberlost. Garden City, NY: Doubleday, Page and Company, 1912.

Friends in Feathers. [Revised and enlarged edition of *What I Have Done with Birds.*] Garden City, NY: Doubleday, Page and Company, 1917.

Homing with the Birds. Garden City, NY: Doubleday, Page and Company, 1919.

Wings. Garden City, NY: Doubleday, Page and Company, 1923. Selected and edited chapters from previous books.

Tales You Won't Believe. Garden City, NY: Doubleday, Page and Company, 1925.

Gene Stratton-Porter's Poetry

The Fire Bird. Garden City, NY: Doubleday, Page and Company, 1922.

Jesus of the Emerald. Garden City, NY: Doubleday, Page and Company, 1923.

"Euphorbia" was never published in book form. It appeared in *Good Housekeeping* January through March 1923.

Miscellany by Gene Stratton-Porter

After the Flood. Indianapolis: Bobbs-Merrill, 1911. Collection of children's stories printed for the Indiana Society of Chicago.

Birds of the Limberlost: Especially Prepared for Miss Katharine Minahan. Garden City, NY: Doubleday, Page and Company, 1914. Sketch for a New York actress who had a talent for imitating the songs of birds.

Morning Face. Garden City, NY: Doubleday, Page and Company, 1916. Children's book.

Let Us Highly Resolve. Garden City, NY: Doubleday, Page and Company, 1927. Collection of essays, mostly reprinted from *McCall's.*

Magazine Articles and Editorials by Gene Stratton-Porter

(Her work appeared more than 170 times in magazines. Below is a select list; articles reprinted in her books are not noted here.)

"All Together, Heave!" *Izaak Walton League Monthly* (December 1922).

"My Work and My Critics." *The Bookman* [London] (February 1916).

"Why I Always Wear My Rose-Colored Glasses." *American Magazine* (August 1919).

"What My Father Meant to Me." *American Magazine* (February 1925).

"Why I Wrote 'A Girl of the Limberlost.'" *World's Work* (February 1910).

Book Contribution by Gene Stratton-Porter

Squier, Emma Lindsay. *The Wild Heart.* New York: Cosmopolitan, 1922. Opening by Gene Stratton-Porter titled "An introduction which might better be entitled: Some youngsters find the wrong parents."

INDEX

Page numbers in italics refer to illustrations